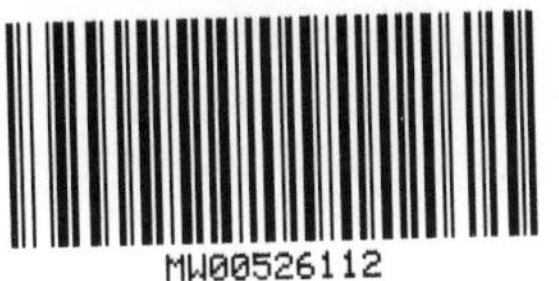

JONAH

A Tale of Mercy

Jimmy A. Long

Ansley and John —
The Lord is
good and
His mercies
endure forever.

Torchflame Books
An imprint of Light Messages

Jonah - A Tale of Mercy
Jimmy A. Long
www.jimmylong.net
jimmy@jimmylong.net

Published 2016, by Torchflame Books
an Imprint of Light Messages
www.lightmessages.com
Durham, NC 27713 USA
SAN: 920-9298

Paperback ISBN: 978-1-61153-211-1
Hardcover ISBN: 978-1-61153-219-7
Ebook ISBN: 978-1-61153-212-8

This work would not have happened without the prayers and support of my church family at Grace Fellowship. It has been a long process for such a short book, but your encouragement kept me moving forward. I appreciate those who took the time to read this story and offer valuable input: Kim McCarter, Germaine Copeland, Ingrid Giller, Donna London, and Tommi Ward. No expression of appreciation would be complete without thanking my family. Nancy, Jackie, and Jay, you have blessed me in ways beyond words. And, finally, I am grateful to God, who has shown me mercy.

Contents

PREFACE

A real man with a real struggle - this is the story of Jonah. As I began to write this little book, I recognized that Jonah's story was not just a fish tale. In those four little chapters, we see a real man wrestle with the call of God in his life. We catch just a glimpse of the anguish of this prophet who was unable to comprehend how God could show mercy to people who were unmerciful. We watch as this faithful man of God abandons all in an attempt to escape his mission and the God who entrusted it to him.

The biblical story of Jonah is bare bones. My desire was to fill in the blanks with possibilities. I have tried very hard to stay true to the Bible and to history, yet the characters you will meet and many of the details you will read are fabricated. The intent is not to change or distort the story. The intent is to paint the picture of a real man whose somewhat simplistic view of God, man, sin, and forgiveness was shaken to the core.

I encourage the reader to enjoy the imaginative additions in the book, but to put his or her trust in the biblical text and the God who is revealed there. My hope is that, in some small way, we might all more fully appreciate and celebrate the great mercy of God.

1
The Dream

Jonah sat close to the fire on an unusually cool night. "I had another dream last night," he said, swallowing a mouthful of fish.

"Like the others?" asked Abidan. He did not like to hear these stories. They were all the same – fear, blood, death. But he had to hear them. He had committed himself to the Lord and to this prophet and one day hoped to inherit the mantle of Jonah – hoped and feared.

Jonah squeezed his eyes shut and swallowed hard, "Yes – like the others." He paused and then began, his eyes wide open but staring at nothing.

"I heard the sound first - a rumbling, deep, constant, ominous. The sound grew deafening, and then I felt it. The ground quivering beneath my feet as grains of sand danced to some strange, unearthly drumming.

It was hot, stifling to be so early. I squinted toward the rising sun. There – I could almost make it out. Something dark. Something coming. I began to quiver like the sand at my feet for I knew. I knew what it was.

I turned to run, but the sand beneath my feet became soft, yielding to my steps, slowing my desperate retreat. 'No. This cannot be! Lord, no! More time, please, more time.'

The sand pulled at my feet, and I fell. I threw my staff aside and reached to catch myself. My hands did not plunge into coarse, scorching sand. The ground was a sticky crimson. I stared, astonished, at my hands. Blood. The ground around me was covered with the same hot, red stickiness.

The rumbling was deafening – then it stopped. All was silent save for my heart pounding in my chest. It was quiet and then went dark. The blinding sun was enveloped in darkness. Was it over? I turned slowly, dreading what horror awaited my gaze. I should never have looked. My blood turned cold.

There it was before me, standing among an army that stretched north to south across the horizon. It was massive, imposing, the height of three of Solomon's temples. It had the body of a strong, sturdy bull, the wings of an eagle spread wide hiding the rising sun, and the head of a man, the face twisted in anger. Its rage erupted into a vicious roar. Blood stained its teeth and ran down the long, black beard. Scattered about it were bodies, lifeless and torn to shreds. Its hooves ground human bones into the bloodstained sand.

The eyes of the monster towering above caught sight of me and narrowed. Its head came closer. I could not run. I could not move held fast in the blackening pool of blood around me and by my own fear. The breath of the beast carried the stench of death. 'Oh, God of my fathers, unworthy as I am, have mercy on me.'

Its teeth were sharp as spears. Its putrid breath sickening as its gaping jaws opened to consume me. Darkness overwhelmed me. I screamed … then I woke drenched with my own sweat, heart racing.

I don't know, Abidan. Was it just a dream? A nightmare? A vision? I can't get it out of my mind. That cursed beast haunts me."

Abidan reached his hand to grasp Jonah's shoulder. He could feel Jonah trembling. "God must be speaking to you. It's just the same. It's always the same."

Jonah gazed at the fire. "Nineveh," he spoke softly and then pulled his robe tightly about him and lay down to sleep. "Lord, God of my fathers, not tonight."

2
The Prophet

Again, Jonah dreamed, but not of blood and monsters. He dreamed of a day that seemed so long ago, the day when he met Yael. It was awkward, almost comical. A prophet of God who could stand before a king or quiet an angry mob, but who could not muster the courage to ask Merari for permission to marry his daughter. "Be bold. Be bold. Be bold," he repeated silently to himself.

As he threw back the purple flap and entered Merari's tent, his mouth went dry. He sat when invited and tried desperately to remember the speech he had so carefully prepared. Jonah knew Yael was standing just outside the tent. She was always so curious, so bold.

"Merari, you are a noble merchant and much respected here. You fear God but fear no man. I am a humble servant of the Most High. When He calls me to speak, I speak. What He calls me to say, I say. I do not come here as a prophet but as a man." The rest of the words were hazy. Jonah talked but did not feel he controlled his words. Would Merari think him a fool?

When Jonah was done, Merari stood. Jonah stood, as well. The merchant stepped toward the tent flap. All was lost. Jonah's heart sank. The flap was thrown open, and Jonah turned to leave. As he neared the exit, Merari's stone cold expression transformed. He grinned and took Jonah by the shoulders. He embraced him and kissed him. "In seven days, my son, we will celebrate your wedding. You can wait that long, can't you?" Merari laughed. It was loud, almost shockingly so, but genuine. Jonah laughed, too. Was he laughing out of joy or relief? He did not know. It did not matter. They laughed and embraced.

"Are you well, Master?" The voice was familiar, but Jonah kept laughing. "You are dreaming. Wake up!" Merari disappeared. The tent disappeared. The laughing stopped.

Jonah opened his eyes slowly. "Ah, it's you. Abidan. There are some dreams I wish would never end." Jonah breathed in deeply, and the bliss of the dream began to fade, being washed away by the heaviness of the appointment they had to keep.

"It's time," said Abidan. His look was serious. His head dropped as if some great weight had been placed on his neck. "We must go."

Slowly, Jonah rolled over and got to his feet. "The donkey is packed," Abidan noted. "We have water and food and wine. You may want to eat a little bread before we travel."

Jonah's mind began to clear. No more laughter, not today. They would be back in Gath-hepher a few hours before dark. Merari would be there, as would his whole clan. Jonah had no one to bring now, except Abidan, but at least he had Abidan. He turned to look at him, his son with dark, curly hair and light brown eyes. He looked like his mother. He looked so much like Yael. There would indeed be no laughter. Jonah wiped a tear from his eye. "I cannot eat, son. Let us go to your mother's grave."

And now Jonah stood in front of the same tent that had been so real in his dream the night before. The once intense purple had faded, but he could never forget this tent. It was the place of laughter and the place of tears. He remembered the first time he entered, and he remembered seven years ago this day sitting with Merari, mourning Yael. Then, his father-in-law was still prosperous. The Assyrian raiding parties had only begun to attack his caravans. Today, the faded purple was a sure indication that the raids had taken an awful toll.

Jonah's face showed a brief smile that faded quickly. "They call me a prophet, but you seem quite adept at knowing who is standing outside your tent," he replied. "It is good to see you father Merari." The older man did not stand, so Jonah went over, stooped down and embraced him, kissing both his cheeks and tasting the salt of recent tears on his graying beard.

As Jonah went back to take his seat among the pillows and blankets, he noticed little had changed in his father-in-law's tent, yet it seemed far smaller and less grand. Merari, too, appeared less grand. He tried to make up for the depletion of his wealth by stacking more pillows beneath himself as he sat, but the attempt made him almost pitiable.

"You look well, Merari." It was only partly true, and they both knew it.

From atop his fringed pile, Merari morbidly quipped, "I am an empty ostrich shell, my son. I am glad you have come. You, especially you, can share this crushing burden. I can still hear her laugh," he paused and looked down, "but I also hear her scream."

Jonah was silent as Merari's thoughts drifted backward through time. It had been a dry day and very windy. The caravans had arrived without being harassed, and there was great joy as donkeys carrying spices, silks, purple cloth, and gold came lumbering into the camp. "No sign of raiders?" Merari asked Jethuel, his only son.

A broad grin stretched across Jethuel's face, and he thumped his chest in feigned pride. "Not with Jethuel, son of Merari, on guard." They both laughed. It was good to laugh.

Jethuel slid down off his horse and embraced his father. "I think the tide is turning," Jethuel spoke with a hint of confidence. "I hear rumors that Egypt wants to break the back of the Assyrians. Perhaps, they are holed up in Nineveh worried about Pharaoh's chariots and archers."

"Perhaps they are worried about Jethuel the braggart," replied his father. "Unload the animals. I will tell the women to prepare a feast. Go take your nephew whatever trinket you brought back this time and ask Yael when Jonah is to return. He left only days after you did, and I worry that he said something to anger King Jeroboam. God gives him words, but I wish the Lord had also given him better sense." Merari turned back toward his tent.

It had seemed only to be a few moments before the screaming started. Chaos broke out in the camp and the servants came to whisk the old patriarch away to safety. Merari insisted they let him stand and fight, but they were unyielding. "No, Lord, Master Jethuel gave us strict orders in these cases. He will muster the fighting men. We must go. Hurry!" And so the last sounds he heard were shouts and screams and steel against steel as he was rushed toward the security of the hills.

Merari remembered it all far too clearly - the haunting sound of women wailing the deaths of sons and husbands, the sight of blood staining the ground all around the tents, and the smell of smoke and of death. He remembered Jethuel's bitter tears and his lament that he could not save his sister. He remembered Abidan's return from hiding in the hills, the way the young boy walked like a lost soul back into the camp. He remembered the emptiness in the boy's eyes, eyes that suddenly came to life with tears at the sight of his grandfather. He remembered how tightly his grandson held to him. He remembered the boy's unbridled sobs, and he remembered his own.

The vividness of that day receded into a sad and dark place in the old man's mind. "I'm sorry, Jonah. I often get lost in the memories," Merari finally spoke again. "Is the boy with you?"

"Yes," Jonah answered, "he went to see his uncle. I asked him to help Jethuel walk to the grave. We should go before dark."

The winds were calm, and the temperatures were beginning to cool by the time they reached the mouth of the cave. Every year since Yael died, they had come to remember. What they wanted to remember was her life, her vitality, her smile and her eyes, but they could not escape the memories of the raid, nor could they forget the empty stare of her once vibrant eyes.

Merari tried to speak. He always tried to honor his precious daughter by telling stories of her life. He never finished even one before being overcome by grief and uncontrollable sobbing. They stood there quietly lost in memories, telling stories only to themselves. The sound of soft crying intermingled with the song of a woodlark.

Abidan stood between his grandfather and his uncle, helping to hold Jethuel steady. This grave was not the only reminder Jethuel had of that day. His right leg was stiff and numb and nearly useless, an unwanted memento from the unexpected raid. The Assyrian marauders had not attacked the caravan on the road because they wanted an even more lucrative haul. They had followed Jethuel, weaving their way through the wadis concealed in the dry channels that flowed with water only during the rainy season.

Jethuel remembered the day with crystal clarity. The servants had been unloading the donkeys after returning from their successful trading venture. Jethuel reached into the bag on his horse and pulled out an intricately carved animal. The wood was dark and rich. The weight of it was surprisingly heavy for something he could hold in his palm. The trader had told him the carving was of an elephant, a massive creature with fierce tusks. The trader had purchased it in Ethiopia and kept talking about how rare it was. Jethuel knew he paid too much, but the expression on Abidan's face would be worth it at twice the price.

With the little African treasure in hand, Jethuel made his way across the camp. As he neared Jonah's tent, he heard what sounded like the thunder of hooves. He turned into the wind but could see only dust above the tents. Was it only the wind and sand? Then he heard the shouts, followed by screams.

The spear had come from nowhere but found its mark in the back of Jethuel's thigh. He went down hard. All he could think was that he didn't want to drop the elephant. He wondered why he would think such a thing given the circumstances, but a jolt of pain yanked him back to reality. He felt the warmth of blood saturating his robes, but the thought of his family dying at the hands of Assyrian dogs held the pain at bay.

He reached around and yanked the spear out. He tried to stand. His right leg would not respond. He grabbed the spear so he would not be completely defenseless. Then he saw him - Abidan, his beloved nephew and the only grandchild of Merari - Abidan, the son of a prophet with the face of an angel.

"Run, Abidan!" Jethuel shouted. "Get your mother and run! Go for the hills, boy! Don't stare at me! Go! Go!" But Abidan didn't run. He stood there eyes fixed on his uncle, oblivious to the noise and chaos around him. He stared with unblinking eyes at Jethuel's agonized face. Abidan's eyes followed a trickle of blood running from a gash on his uncle's forehead and down his cheek. His blank eyes drifted downward toward Jethuel's left hand and a brief, puzzled look registered as he noticed something there - black, carved - and Jethuel screamed again,"Abidan, please! Get your mother! Run!"

As if awakened from a trance, Abidan's expression had transformed from wonder to fear. He disappeared behind the tent flap and emerged in a moment with his mother's hand fastened tightly in his own. Immediately, Yael saw her brother in the bloodstained dirt. She jerked free of Abidan and ran to Jethuel.

"No! The thieves followed us here. You must go now," shouted her brother. She hesitated, mid-stride, and turned to do as her brother beckoned. She never took another step.

From her left had bounded one of the Assyrian raiders, his blade drawn, a twisted smile on his face. He ran swiftly and swung his sword. Yael did not see him as the blade buried deeply into her back. She reached toward Abidan, but her legs would not carry her to him. She fell hard. Jethuel watched her grasping at the dirt. Her lips moved. He could not hear her words above the clamor, but he knew the words she formed on her lips. He had seen them utter the words many times. "Hear, O Israel, the Lord your God, the Lord is one." Did she smile? Was it his imagination? Then, all movement stopped.

Fear overcame him, and Abidan ran. The Assyrian paid no attention to him but turned his attention to the man struggling to regain his feet. Jethuel saw his sister's murderer striding toward him. As the raider raised his sword for the kill, Jethuel closed his eyes and began to pray, but the sword did not fall. Instead, he felt a tugging at his hand. He opened his eyes to see the murderer taking the little wooden elephant from his hand. He thought it strange the savage would hesitate for a toy. He fully expected the Assyrian's next move would be to plunge his sword into the heart of his helpless victim. As Jethuel prepared to join his sister in the grave, he heard shouts and, to his surprise, saw the raider turn and run. The loss of blood overcame him, and the lifeless body of Yael was the last sight Jethuel saw before drifting into unconsciousness. Now, seven years later, he was still lost in the pain of that awful day.

They had all come to that solemn place brimming with memories, but as they stood before the stone covering the cave where Yael's body had been placed, each was silent. Of course, it was always this way. No one could find the words, and those who had words could not speak them. It always came back to the man of God doing what men of God do, so Jonah prayed. Night fell, and they slowly made their way back to the tents.

3
The Call

Early the next morning, Jonah woke from a dreamless sleep. How long had it been since he was spared either the monsters or lost love? He tied his sandals, stood to put on his outer robe, and slid through the tent's opening. He was greeted by a cool breeze and the sounds of cattle and sheep in their pens. The pre-dawn sky was dark. The stars twinkled like brilliant diamonds against that inky background, but Jonah paid little attention. He was on a mission, his own very personal one. With staff in hand, Jonah made his way back to the cave where the bones of his beloved wife lay.

He sat heavily on a rock. The intense sadness of the previous day was lifted. He did not come to talk to Yael. She was in Abraham's bosom, safe, and Jonah longed for the day they would reunite. He had come early this morning to talk with his God and to listen for His voice. He had learned long ago that noise and busyness were enemies of hearing God's voice. Here, it would be quiet.

"God of my fathers, Almighty One, King of Heaven and Earth, Redeemer of Israel, I am your humble servant. I do not come to ask for blessings. I come to ask you to speak to me again. I grow weary of the dreams. I don't know what you mean or what you want. I know in my dreams you are speaking to me, but I don't know what you are trying to say. I want to know what these terrible visions mean. Be merciful to me. Speak, Lord. I listen for your voice."

Silence. Three times Jonah prepared to get up and walk away, but an unseen hand kept him seated on the rock. The wind blew harder as the first hints of sunrise could be seen over the hills.

"Jonah."

Jonah's eyes darted upward. He cocked his head and listened more intently. This time the voice came louder, "Jonah."

"I am here, Lord," the eager prophet replied. The voice spoke softly, tenderly, but with great authority. It was unmistakable – the voice of God. Jonah caught himself holding his breath in anticipation.

"Jonah, get up."

Jonah stood as he had so many times before. He cherished the voice of God, though His words were often a burden. Jonah had spoken severe messages of judgment to Israel's king, but the prophet had also carried promises of victory and success. Long ago, he had decided to go wherever the Lord told him to go and to speak whatever words the Lord gave him to speak. He never wavered from speaking God's words faithfully. Jonah steadied himself for whatever message the Lord would have him deliver. He was prepared to go and to speak...until the word came.

"Jonah, go to Nineveh."

Jonah stood still, waiting for something more, something that would explain this word from God. Nothing more came. "Lord, not Nineveh. I cannot go there. I cannot go. I will not...." His words trailed off into silence, and Jonah just stood there as the sun crept over the hills, and the winds began to blow harder. He stood against the wind, the sand stinging his face. He stood hoping God would relent. When his eyes became dry, he closed them tightly, but still he stood. It was his stance of resistance.

This was how Jonah stood when King Jeroboam ranted and raged at him from the throne. This was how he stood when the people in the streets of Samaria shouted at him as he decried their moral corruption. The King of Israel always relented. The people of Jeroboam's kingdom always dispersed and went home grumbling. It was Jonah, the righteous prophet of God, who remained standing.

The sun had risen above the distant hills. Jonah could see the brightness of it through his tightly closed eyes. Grains of sand peppered his lips that were now dry and painfully sensitive. Jonah had gambled that he could make this defiant stance against the Almighty One, but it was not the King of heaven who would relent this day; it was His prophet.

Jonah sank to the ground and pulled his cloak over himself to protect his chaffed face from the sandstorm. "Nineveh," he whispered to himself. The word was like acid churning in his knotted stomach.

He shifted his cloak a bit and peeked out to see the morning's light brightening the hefty stone covering the entrance to the cave that concealed the remains of Yael. His feeling of dismay over the Lord's command was now accompanied by an overwhelming, burning anger. This place, this grave was the work of Nineveh. What those Assyrian dogs had stolen from Jonah was infinitely precious. In spite of the years that had passed, the loss was still just as painful. It was a burden that seemed to only grow heavier.

With visions of fire and brimstone raining down from heaven on that city, Jonah spoke to himself, "Nineveh. Perhaps God is giving me the favor of telling you that your time is over. Perhaps God is allowing me to witness your execution. Dogs!" Jonah spat on the ground. He could feel the burning of bile rising in his throat.

Jonah stood and turned his back on Yael's tomb. He was restless as he began his walk back to the camp. The winds had calmed, and the grains of sand no longer ripped at his exposed face. His steps were slow, his eyes staring at the path just ahead of him. He had wanted so desperately to hear God's voice, but in hearing this divine call Jonah became a conflicted man.

A debate raged inside Jonah as he traversed his way along the path. He mindlessly stepped over rocks and ducked his head to avoid tree limbs. "I have never stood in defiance against the Lord. What kind of fool am I? Why did I go there to hear from Him? That place is filled with too many memories, too much pain. Why did God not preserve Yael's life? I was doing His work. Was it too much to ask that He look after my family?"

The years raced through Jonah's mind. He saw the smile on Merari's face as he placed Yael's hand in Jonah's, his bride's face radiant with joy. He heard her laughter like a song playing in his soul. He saw her holding Abidan so tenderly. And Jonah saw her standing with their young boy as the determined prophet climbed on his donkey to go once more and deliver a word from God to the king.

If only the memories could end there - If he could somehow go back to that time, he would never have left Merari's camp. If he had been there, perhaps Yael might still be alive. But Jonah's mind carried him further. He saw Merari looking frail and old. Jonah saw his lips moving, forming words that tore at the prophet's heart. "I am sorry, my son," Merari's voice cracked, "Yael is dead."

"Yael is dead." The words were seared in Jonah's mind. They played over and over like the incessant beat of a drum. Was it even possible? He could almost feel the warmth of her embrace before he left on his journey, the press of her lips against his cheek, the sound of her voice speaking a quiet blessing in his ear. He could see the life in her eyes as the flecks of gold in her deep brown eyes danced in the early morning sunlight. He would never look into those lively, beautiful eyes again.

Yael had been a gentle soul. Her words had soothed Jonah when he was troubled. Her touch melted away the fears and anxieties that plagued him in private moments. Her admiration of him was a source of strength. The image of his beloved filled his mind and swelled his heart. It was almost as if she were there.

"Master?" A distant voice penetrated the fog of Jonah's reverie. "Father, are you all right?"

Jonah was pulled back into reality. It was Abidan, looking deeply concerned, standing outside their tent. "Are you ill, father?" Abidan asked with a look of concern.

"No, my son, I am fine. I needed to get away and pray," Jonah answered.

Abidan's eyes widened. "He spoke to you, didn't He?" he asked.

Jonah swallowed hard. He could feel the bile rising again and the burning in his throat. "Yes, Abidan, the Lord spoke."

"Did He give you a word to speak?" his son asked, expectantly. Jonah did not answer. He had not fully grasped why the Lord might send a messenger to Nineveh, that wicked and vile city. Why not just rain fire down from heaven? Why not just leave that city and all its citizens as a pile of ashes to be scattered in the wind? Let them be like Sodom and Gomorrah. Why the warning at all? Did the raiders warn Jethuel they were following him? Did the murderer warn Yael before he struck?

Jonah looked into Abidan's face and could see Yael in him. He softened his voice. "I cannot tell you what the Lord spoke to me," started Jonah. "I am not sure I understand what He wants. Go and get your uncle. Bring him to your grandfather's tent. I will meet them there in a moment."

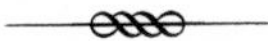

When Jonah entered his father-in-law's tent, he sent Abidan out. "Go. Get my things together. I will be leaving today," he told his son.

"And where did the Lord say we will go?" Abidan asked.

Placing his hand on his son's shoulders Jonah said simply, "I must go alone."

Abidan's face fell with the news, but he turned and started on his assigned task. His father had often made such a statement, but Abidan's insistence frequently wore his father down. He would wait and plead his case later.

As Abidan left, Jonah sat down across from Merari. Jonah's eyes looked down at the intricate pattern woven into the pillow in front of him. He traced his finger along a golden thread. Taking a long, deep breath, Jonah began. "This morning the Lord spoke to me. He is sending me...," Jonah hesitated, "He is sending me to Nineveh." Merari's eyes grew wide. Jethuel's mouth opened to speak, but he made no sound.

For a long agonizing moment, there was only silence in the tent. Jethuel was the first to speak, "Nineveh...so God has heard my prayers and is bringing judgment on the dogs." His face expressed precisely the pain and anger in his heart. "Let them burn. Let them suffer."

Merari said nothing. He only looked thoughtfully at Jonah as if he were peering into the prophet's soul. Jonah asked, "And what say you?" Merari had always provided wise counsel, even when his words were less than comforting.

"My son," the aging merchant began, "you have stood before kings and priests and common men. You have spoken faithfully the words God gives you. You have warned men to turn from their wickedness or God would bring upon them the punishment they so justly deserved. What if...." Merari's voice drifted into nothingness.

Jonah did not need to hear him finish. He knew how that sentence would end. Jonah completed it, "What if the people repent, and the Lord withholds His judgment? What if He shows mercy?"

"He would not!" shouted Jetheul as he struggled to his feet. "He cannot! They steal and slaughter indiscriminately. They skin men alive merely for sport. They do not acknowledge the Lord but worship idols." His face reddened and his eyes fixed on Jonah. "And they killed Yael!" His voice became a plea, "Jonah, they killed Yael." Tears streamed down Jethuel's face.

Jonah rose slowly to his feet and walked over to Merari. He bent down, hugged, and kissed him. Straightening himself, he turned to Jethuel and placed a strong hand on his shoulder. Jonah spoke to his brother-in-law, "Look after Abidan. I will be away for some time. He does not need to know where I am going, or he may follow. Jethuel, do not tell him where I am going," he spoke with authority.

Jethuel lifted his eyes, and the two men stood looking at one another, Jonah trying to find some hint that Yael's dear brother understood. "Perhaps," Jonah continued, "I will be able to bring you a handful of ashes from Nineveh to make up for your leg." And with that, Jonah walked out into the blinding sunlight.

He had given instructions for the servants to pack supplies. Two donkeys were tied to a post near Jonah's tent. Abidan sat a few feet away in the shade. He stood when he caught sight of his father.

"Master, the Lord must be sending us on a long journey. Will we go to Jerusalem?" the young Abidan asked hopefully.

"No. We will not be going to Jerusalem, my child," Jonah said without emotion. "I have been called by God and must leave immediately. I am afraid that this time you cannot go with me. Besides, you have been away from your grandfather and uncle too long. Jethuel's limp is getting worse, and Merari is no longer a young calf. They will find ample work for you to do here. I am leaving the scrolls; study them. Read them aloud to your grandfather. He will like that. Remember, these words are life to you. They reveal the heart and will of God. They will guide you like a lamp in the darkness." Jonah's words were gentle and encouraging, but even as he spoke them, he recognized that his tone seemed to be but a thin coat of whitewash concealing something left unspoken.

"But…" Abidan began. Jonah turned and placed both his hands firmly on his son's shoulders, quieting him. The shoulders beneath the robes were strong. Abidan had grown into a young man full of curiosity and ready for adventure, but this would not be his adventure. This was a journey Jonah must make alone.

"I will come to you soon," Jonah said and kissed Abidan on each cheek. "We will make plans to go to Jerusalem or to Sinai if the Lord is willing."

“Father, you have prayed for me many times,” Abidan said, “and you have taught me to pray. Do me the honor of letting me pray for you.” Jonah paused briefly, then nodded for his son to continue.

Abidan raised his eyes to the sky. “Lord, God of my fathers, Creator of the land and the sea and all that is in them, I ask you this day to strengthen your servant. Speak words of truth through him. Empower him to stand boldly before kings and false prophets. Do not forsake him in the night, and please shelter him in the day. May he be Your chosen vessel guided by Your Spirit, just as a ship is carried along by the strong wind. May He find Your mercy for himself and declare to all that You are a merciful God. And, Lord, bring him safely back to me. Amen.”

Father and son shared a brief smile. Then, Abidan untied the donkeys and placed the ropes in his father’s hand. Thus, Jonah began his journey to that great and wicked city.

Somewhere in the din of the camp, he heard a woman’s laugh. “Yael,” he thought immediately, as his skin tingled and his heart raced, but reality soon recaptured his mind, and he sighed. The words Merari had spoken that dreadful day fell softly and sadly from Jonah’s lips, “Yael is dead.”

After a brief and sorrowful moment, he added, “And I go to preach to those responsible for murdering her.” Jonah’s eyes became moist, and a tear rolled down his cheek as his donkey plodded along the worn path.

4

The Struggle

The sun cast long shadows as Jonah stepped through the gates of Jabneel. He heard the shouts of children playing and a mother calling out somewhere up ahead. It would soon be dark, and the weary prophet would find a place to stay for the night.

Jonah walked with his two donkeys down a long street. The evening wind created dirt devils spinning and dying like a half-hearted welcoming party. Two men and a boy came walking briskly toward him, seemingly on their way somewhere they considered important. They spoke in excited terms but so quickly Jonah could not make out what they were saying.

"Pardon me," Jonah spoke interrupting their hurried conversation. "I am looking for a place to stay for the night, an inn, perhaps, and a place for my animals."

The three stopped and they turned in unison toward him. The older man spoke first. "You are a Jew, yes?" he inquired.

"I am," Jonah answered, "and a prophet of the Most High."

The eyes of all three men widened. They bowed slightly in his presence, and the boy asked, "Lodging? There are many places here, but the food is terrible. No one cooks like my mother." He turned to the older man and asked excitedly, "Father, can the prophet come to our house? We have room."

The look from the older man made it clear to Jonah he would likely have to continue his search for a place to stay. "Come," said the man, ignoring Jonah and speaking only to his two companions, "we will be late for dinner." He turned his face away and began to walk on his original course and with nearly the same pace. The other two remained standing in their spots, looking somewhat confused, but did not argue. With an apologetic look toward Jonah, the son stepped around him and moved to follow his father. Their companion fell in step behind the two.

Jonah continued his way, looking from side to side and hoping to find some sign that he had found a good place for the night. He had traveled thirty or so steps when he heard someone rushing up behind him. The footsteps stopped short of Jonah to avoid startling the donkeys.

Jonah turned to see the young man once more. "I am Arieh. I am sorry for my father's rudeness. He has asked me to invite you to come to our home. We will gladly provide for your needs and those of your animals. You will be safe and well fed. Come," the young man motioned. "It's not far. Let me have the ropes so that you do not have to hold the donkeys. They can be stubborn, yes? You're a prophet! That is so exciting. What does the Lord sound like? Is there fire or smoke? Reuben will not believe a real prophet stayed in our house! Can I invite him?"

Jonah took in a deep breath as Arieh continued. It would not be a quiet night.

The boy walked with Jonah out the same gate the weary prophet had entered. Arieh talked the entire way to the modest home that stood just outside the town's walls. The smell of olive oil was strong. Jonah could make out the silhouette of a winepress just off to his left.

Arieh took the donkeys and headed toward a makeshift barn some hundred or so paces away. "I'll get them water and fodder and close them in for the night. Don't worry," the boy added, "I'll bring your supplies inside." He motioned to the blanket covering the doorway. "Please go in. Oh, I almost forgot - my father's name is Chesed."

"Chesed," Jonah thought to himself. "We'll see if he is as merciful as his name implies."

Jonah walked toward the house and pulled back the blanket to step in. "May the mercy and peace of God be on this house for all generations," Jonah spoke as he bowed his head. All eyes had turned toward him as he stood in the doorway.

"Come. Sit," Chesed spoke. He called for a young female servant who removed the sandals from Jonah's feet and began to wash away the dust. She never lifted her eyes to meet his. She rose, taking Jonah's sandals with her. She placed them near the doorway and then retreated with her bowl toward the back of the house.

The place was sparsely appointed. Blankets were placed in the center of the main room where Chesed sat with the other man Jonah had seen earlier. Flames danced atop three lamps near the back wall. Jonah thought their placement was intentional. Jonah's face would be lighted while his host's face would remain shaded. It was very likely this man had been deceived by strangers before.

Jonah sought to put Chesed's mind at ease. "I am grateful to you for allowing me to stay here. I will be no trouble." He paused, and then added, "If you wish, I can sleep with my animals in the barn." The response was immediate.

"Nonsense!" Chesed barked, the expression of his face concealed by dark shadows. "You will sleep here, or on the roof if you prefer. I would not invite the Lord's judgment on me for refusing a man of God. My wife has prepared a young goat. You will not find a finer cook in all of Jabneel." Chesed paused and turned toward his companion, "Ah, forgive me. Where are my manners? This is my future son-in-law, Hiram." Jonah nodded in the man's direction.

The blanket over the doorway was swept back revealing Arieh carrying an armload of supplies which he sat down roughly just inside the opening. The look on his face was one of surprise, as if he really didn't expect Jonah to be in the house. "Everything is set. Oh, I dropped one of the wineskins. It tore. I am so very sorry, but I will replace it with two." Arieh's eyes jumped from

Jonah to his father, and when their eyes met, the life in his face drained away. His speech stuttered, "I, uh…"

Chesed did not wait for him to finish. "Go help the women," he said to Arieh in a tone that let Jonah know there would be a longer conversation later. The boy disappeared behind another blanket hanging to Jonah's right. "I am sorry," Chesed said. "He tries. He is over-eager, perhaps, in the presence of so great a man." Jonah detected some bitterness in his voice.

The meal came soon after, and Jonah, hungry, ate heartily. The food was served by the same girl who had washed his feet earlier. The goat was roasted to perfection, and all three ate generously. Arieh did not come to dinner, and there was little conversation between the three men. Jonah had expected many questions from his host, questions which he did not wish to answer. Eating the meal in silence was a welcome relief.

As they finished their meal, Hiram spoke his first words, "Tell me. What brought you here? Did God send you to this place?" There was a hint of anxiety in his voice.

"No. I am passing through. The Lord has given me no message for this house or this village," Jonah spoke, hoping to reassure both men. He drank deeply of the wine in his cup. It was sweet, much sweeter than most. This was surely the best in the house.

Hiram seemed to lose some of the tenseness that had marked his face. Jonah was still unable to read the shadowed face of his host. Chesed was a shrewd businessman or had been at one time.

Chesed rose suddenly. "Let us walk," he said. He placed a hand on Hiram's shoulder to keep him seated. "Girl!" Chesed yelled. The servant girl appeared once more, head bowed toward her master. He pointed his finger at Jonah's feet and then at the doorway. She quickly went to fetch the sandals she had placed there earlier and rushed to Jonah before he could stand. She wrapped the leather and tied it securely, and then picked up another pair of sandals from a woven basket and put them on Chesed's feet.

Jonah stood and Chesed guided him to the doorway. They moved the blanket aside and stepped into the night's inky blackness. They circled the house and headed toward the fire. The greasy spit that had held the goat as it was cooked was propped against the house. The smell was nearly as delightful as the meat had tasted.

"Sit," Chesed motioned to a pile of straw covered by a blanket. Jonah did. As the evening's chill had set in, he was grateful for the warmth of the fire. Chesed turned to him, asking, "Why are you really here?" This time his host's face was well lit as the flames leapt and danced between the men. There was no anger in his face, only genuine curiosity.

Jonah sat and thought of how to tell his host the Lord was sending him to Nineveh. Surely that would sound insane. No prophet had ever been called to travel to a pagan city to preach. If Chesed had any doubts about Jonah's credibility, this would surely reinforce them.

"I mean you no disrespect, Chesed. You have shown a weary traveler mercy this day. I wish to honor you, but the message of the Lord was not for you or your household."

Chesed poked the fire causing sparks to scramble into the sky. "Urmitu," he spoke, "you may come out." A woman emerged from the house. She moved slowly toward the fire. "Come, wife. Sit. Tell the prophet what you dreamed last night."

The woman's features were fair, and she walked with grace. She must have been at least twenty years younger than her husband. She covered her head as she sat down near Chesed. She spoke without passion. "I saw you, man of God, but you were in a large city. All around you was darkness and wickedness. You opened your mouth and light emerged. It pushed back the darkness. It fled from you." She stopped.

"Go on," Chesed nudged her. "Tell him all of it."

She continued. "I saw another man. He was covered with darkness. You spoke, and the darkness lost its grip on him. The man stood there with a sword in his hand. He was bloody. The blood dripped from his fingertips and formed puddles around him. He held out the sword to you as he knelt in the pool of blood and bowed his head. You took the sword. You were weeping, man of God, great sorrowful cries. You raised the sword to strike him. The darkness began to dance and pulse around you. Then I heard a voice speaking, 'Mercy.' You did not strike the man; though you wanted to, you did not. I still see the dream vividly, but I do not know what it means."

"Do you know of what she speaks, Prophet?" Chesed spoke with a new gentleness in his voice. "She woke up screaming my name over and over again. It was not until she could tell me her dream that I understood it wasn't my name she was speaking of, but of mercy itself."

Jonah looked up from the fire and caught sight of Urmitu's eyes. They were an unusual emerald color. "The city in your dream - have you seen this city before?" he asked.

"Yes," she spoke softly and paused. With a slight tremble in her voice, Urmitu spoke, "It is Nineveh."

Jonah closed his eyes and did not speak; instead, he sat lost in thoughts of Yael and Jethuel. The Lord was taking him to the heart of evil to proclaim judgment on a cruel pack of dogs. Judgment was deserved. The fate of Sodom and Gomorrah was far too good for them. The Lord dared not show them mercy. They did not deserve mercy. They deserved pain and destruction and death. Nineveh must burn.

"How do you know? How do you know it was Nineveh?" Jonah spoke, his tone mixed with anger and sorrow.

With eyes staring into the distance, Urmitu responded, "I remember it from when I was a little girl. I am from Nineveh. I had been sold by my parents to pay a debt. The traders were taking me to Egypt or Cush or someplace. We were crossing the Jordan when a fight broke out among the men. I was able to run away in the confusion. Chesed found me. He was tender and kind to me. When he told me that his name meant mercy, I knew the gods had blessed me."

"God!" Chesed corrected firmly. "Forgive her, man of God; she has faith in the Lord, but has a hard time leaving old habits behind."

"The night grows short, and I must leave early in the morning," said Jonah standing.

"You are going to Nineveh?" asked Chesed.

Jonah stopped and turned to face his host, "That is what the Lord has called me to do, but I do not go with a message of mercy, only judgment."

Chesed walked around the fire and leaned in close to Jonah. "I have no wish to see that corrupt and vile city spared. Would that God would wipe out every Assyrian, save Urmitu, I would rejoice. You can preach your message of damnation and well you should, but if the Lord chooses to show mercy, it is His business. Can you or I question His ways? Would it not be like Him to love the utterly unlovable?"

Jonah turned and placed both hands on Chesed's shoulders. "You have been more than kind," he said quietly. "May God bless you and your family. May the olive oil flow like the Jordan from your presses. May your wine always be sweet, and your cup always be full. May your goats and lambs multiply so the men of this city speak of your prosperity." Jonah turned his head and smiled gently at Urmitu, and then moved toward the barn. "I will sleep with the animals. Have your son bring me my packs before dawn. I must leave early."

Urmitu turned her head to catch her husband's attention. He understood her meaning immediately. Chesed responded, "Prophet, you have blessed me. Will you now turn down my hospitality? Is it because of Urmitu, because of her dream?"

"No," came Jonah's answer as he walked away, "I need to be alone."

Chesed reached for his wife's hand and with a final nod in Jonah's direction, they turned and headed into the house. Jonah rearranged the straw and lay down to sleep. He pulled his cloak up to his neck and closed his eyes, but sleep would not be his friend this night. He tried to get the images from his own dreams to disappear. He tried to get the images from Urmitu's dream to disappear. Most of all, he tried to get the image of Yael to disappear. He wanted nothingness. He envied the donkeys sleeping a dreamless sleep, oblivious to all that was taking place around them.

After more than an hour of rearranging his sleeping position and trying to rearrange his thoughts, Jonah finally stood and wrapped his cloak tightly around him. He walked out to the fire, now dying for lack of care. He poked at it with a stick, sending bright flecks of red and orange upward.

"Lord, God of my fathers, I beg You to take this calling from me. Choose some other prophet who does not know the pain inflicted by Nineveh. I know the kind of God You are. Where I would bring fire down upon the head of the Ninevites, You would offer them pardon, forgiveness. How could they deserve forgiveness? They live in disobedience to You. They worship false gods. They slaughter the innocent and tear the skin off their foes. Tell me that You will destroy them - for Your glory - for Yael."

The answer Jonah received was silence. Jonah was familiar with God's silence. It was as powerful and impactful as His voice. His first encounter with the Lord's refusal to speak had come shortly after Jonah was called to be a prophet. As he watched sparks dance among the ashes, Jonah's thoughts drifted to that day.

Jonah's father, Amittai, had been delirious and running a high fever. Only days before Jonah had heard God's voice telling the young man that he would soon stand before the king. Amittai had rejoiced to hear the Lord had called his son. That day, however, he did not even recognize his only child.

Jonah had been sitting before another dying fire. His tears had made streaks through the ashes smeared on his face. He had cried out to the Lord asking that his father's life might be spared, that he might once more hear his father tell stories of Abraham, Issac, and Jacob. Jonah had begged God for a sign. He had pleaded with the Lord to speak again, yet the night remained quiet.

He had wondered how God's word could be so clear and empowering only days before and so absent on that night. Did He not care? Could He not hear Jonah's prayers? Had his father sinned and brought this upon himself? Jonah had been desperate for answers. He had waited for answers. No answers came.

He had heard quiet steps coming toward him. He did not need to look up to see who had made the sound. He knew it was his mother Rebekah. He also knew his father was gone. Jonah stared into the ashes and followed the ribbon of twisting smoke upward toward the stars.

Jonah remembered how his mother had sat close by her son on the old log and the comfort of her arms around him. That night they had wept quietly both for and with each other. As the first traces of dawn had approached, it was not God's voice Jonah heard but that of his mother, "My son, sometimes God is silent…but He is never absent."

"He is silent but not absent," Jonah spoke softly into the empty night as the last of Chesed's embers turned dark. The air was still. The night was cloudless. Jonah felt completely alone.

"What if," he thought, "I do not go? If the people of Nineveh do not hear that the judgment of God is about to fall on them; then, perhaps, there will be no chance for them to repent and no hope of God's mercy. It will mean I must forsake the mantle of a prophet. It will mean that I will not see Abidan again. It will mean…" His thoughts drifted into nothingness.

It was a very long and sleepless night. Jonah was sore and tired. Inwardly, he was felt twisted and knotted up. That which he knew he should do was the one thing he dreaded most. A sense of unworthiness swept over him. Perhaps he had never been worthy of wearing the mantle of a prophet, of speaking words on behalf of God.

Jonah was startled when from behind him, a quiet voice pulled him back into the moment, "Prophet," Arieh whispered. Jonah turned and squinted, his eyes focusing on the young man coming toward him, weighed down with packs and bags. There was excitement in his eyes. Jonah had seen this kind of admiration in many young men. They thought it such an honor to speak for God. They had no idea the heaviness of such a burden. Jonah thought, "Would that I could carry my burden with the enthusiasm that this youth carries his."

Arieh's voice grew louder as he drew closer, "I replaced your torn wineskin with two others, and there is bread and cheese. I would very much like go with you for a while if you'd like. You could tell me of the things you have seen. Do you have children? A wife? Have you stood before kings? Has a king ever threatened you? Do you ever get scared?" He continued to talk as he strapped the packs to the donkeys. He continued to talk as he walked them to the water trough. Perhaps God was silent, but this boy was not, Jonah mused.

"I need to go alone," Jonah told Arieh, sternly, silencing the boy's incessant questioning.

As he brought the donkeys to Jonah, Arieh knelt down before the prophet. "Will you bless me?" he asked earnestly.

After the events of the night, Jonah was taken back by the request. He hesitated for what seemed a long time. Arieh looked up with utter confusion in his eyes. Jonah forced a smile and placed his right hand on the boy's head. He raised the other hand toward heaven. He opened his mouth to speak but could not form the words. He stood there for minutes looking into the still dark sky, now starless and seeming to be utterly empty. Arieh, with his head still bowed, hesitantly asked, "Will you not bless me?" There was a pleading tone in his voice.

Jonah pressed harder on the boy's head. "Bless you, my child," was all that he could think to say. His first attempt was weak, so he said it a second time with all the confidence he could muster, which was, he confessed inwardly, precious little.

Jonah removed his hand from the boy and took the ropes tied to the donkeys' bridles. With a great heaviness in his heart, he began to walk toward the Jordan River, shielding his eyes against the rising sun. The distance should be covered quickly, and then he would find a shallow place and wade through it on his way to Nineveh. The very thought of the city caused bile to rise in this throat.

Jonah looked once back to see Arieh standing there, watching him walk away. The boy had a good heart. He was a bit overeager, but it was likely a bit of his eagerness would wear away as the years passed. Jonah hoped so, for the boy's sake.

Jonah passed through the town of Jabneel as its people were just waking up for a new day. He watched as women started fires, and men gathered their tools for a long day's work ahead of them. He heard the laughter of a child and paused to watch a mother tickling a toddler. In his mind, the scene changed from this unknown woman and child to Yael and Abidan.

Jonah closed his eyes and allowed his mind to drift along with his heart. Abidan had been such a joyful child. His laughter was contagious. He would waddle up to his mother or father or even total strangers and throw his arms up with the expectation that tickling fingers would find their way along his rib cage. It was amazing Yael had been able to get anything done during the day with their little boy begging constantly to be tickled. How often had Jonah lost himself in that laughter?

But there had not been much laughter after that awful day of blood and death. When they did laugh, both Abidan and his father felt that the laughter was strangely out of place, as if they had disrespected something sacred. Undoubtedly, it was the absence of Yael's sweet laughter that made them feel this way.

As he retreated further into that memory, Jonah let his inner gaze drift from his giggling little boy to the wide smile of his wife. He dwelt there a moment, tracing the outline of her lips with his thoughts, and when he reached the corner of her mouth, he was startled when a trickle of blood ran from between her lips. Jonah let out an audible gasp.

The laughter stopped, and Jonah threw open his eyes. The woman looked suspiciously at this man with his donkeys. She picked up her small child and headed back toward her home. Jonah took a deep breath and, once more, began his dreaded trek.

As he neared the Jordan, a gentle breeze stirred Jonah's robes. A voice from behind him startled Jonah. "It's going to be a hot one, man of God." It was Hiram.

"Is everything all right?" Jonah asked.

"Yes, I just needed to speak with you," answered Hiram. He continued, "Are you truly going to Nineveh?"

The two men walked a short distance to a stand of trees. Jonah tied the donkeys to the spindly limb of a tamarisk tree, and the two men sat down at the base of a sturdy poplar. Hiram again asked his question, "Are you going to Nineveh?"

With his eyes cast to the ground, Jonah replied, "Yes." Turning to the younger man Jonah questioned, "Why did you come after me?"

It was Hiram's turn to stare at the ground. "I suppose," he began, "I came to dissuade you. Never have I heard of a prophet of the Most High being sent to a pagan city, and never could I imagine that if the Lord were to send a prophet to a pagan city that it would be Nineveh. Are you certain you must go?"

"I have no choice," Jonah replied. He scooped up a handful of soil and held it up, letting it slip between his fingers. The breeze carried the fine powder downwind. "Does the dust tell the wind which way to blow? Does the fish tell the tide when to retreat and when to advance? Does a man refuse to heed the call of God?"

"But why would the Lord send you to Nineveh?" pleaded Hiram. "I have heard the stories of their evil. They are a people without mercy, and they deserve none. For God to warn them of impending doom may cause some of them to flee for safety." Hiram paused, and then added, "To warn them of the judgment to come might even cause some of them to repent. Chesed says the business of mercy should best be left to God. Prophet, if God wants them warned, then let God Himself do so."

Jonah turned his eyes to meet Hiram's. Hiram spoke slowly, "You do not want to do this. I can see it in your face. You carry a great pain - a pain that would only be multiplied if you do this."

Hiram stood and began to walk back toward Jabneel. He stopped a few paces away and turned back to speak his final words, "You are not the dust, and you are not a fish. You have a choice." Jonah dropped his head into his hands as Hiram walked away.

"A choice," Jonah mumbled to himself. "I have a choice…" He spoke the words and let them drift away, but they did not drift far. They seemed to have a life of their own. The prophet began to let the idea tumble around in his mind. "If I go, God may still judge the dogs," Jonah paused as he contemplated the other awful conclusion, "or He may show mercy." The thought of the

Lord being merciful to the man who killed Yael brought stinging tears to Jonah's eyes.

Jonah stood with his face pointed heavenward. He spoke quietly but could not hide the anguish, "I have never turned my back on Your call, Lord. No matter how dangerous the situation or how difficult the words, I have been faithful. Now, You ask me to go to the land of devils and speak for You. You ask me to forget my pain and forsake the memory of my beloved. Strike me dead, if you must, but I will not go!"

Jonah waited, fully expecting fire to fall down from heaven and consume him on the spot. Nothing happened. No fire. No voice. Nothing. Even the breeze had died down. The rebellious prophet stood in silence, not knowing exactly what to do.

His mind was numb. His legs were weak. Jonah was uncertain where he should go, but he knew he could not stay where he was. He untied the donkeys and began to walk a well-worn path that followed the Jordan southward.

He debated returning to Gath-hepher. The wayward man of God hesitated, his mind playing through multiple scenarios. "Where will I go?" he pondered as he resumed his steps past the olive groves. He turned back to see Arieh, who had obviously followed Jonah at a distance. The boy was simply standing there with a confused look on his face. "Give your father my thanks," Jonah said with a forced smile.

Walking far enough that he escaped Arieh's gaze, Jonah came to a sudden stop. "Joppa," the thought came to him all at once. "I will go to Joppa and sail as far away as possible." Jonah stopped and mounted one of the donkeys. He kicked at the animal's side to increase its pace. "I must leave this place far behind, the place of my decision, the place of my rebellion. Maybe the Lord will be merciful with me." The thought of mercy was no longer sweet and caused his stomach to churn.

5

The Flight

It was still a couple of hours before noon, and the wind carried the salty fragrance of the sea to Jonah. He had traveled six days with only fitful sleep during the nights. The trek had been long, uneventful, and very dusty. He looked forward to the moist air of Joppa.

The once bold prophet had come to terms with his rebellion. His nights had not been interrupted by dreams sent from the Lord, though admittedly, he had not had much sleep, either. There had been no voice from heaven and no signs in the sky. Jonah felt very, very alone. He did not feel like a man who had been abandoned, but as one who had left something precious behind. He was filled with both regret and relief.

Jonah was amazed at how simple it was to turn away from God's call. Ever since he walked away from Yael's tomb, he had pleaded with God not to send him to Nineveh. His pleas were met with only silence. Yael's face constantly haunted his soul. One moment the image of his wife was alive with sparkling eyes and a sweet smile accented by deep dimples. The next moment her face turned ashen gray, and the lips were parted and dry. How could God call him to go to that wicked city? To those wicked people? It was not fair! It was just too much to ask a man who had lost so much. God was wrong.

Even the thought that God might be wrong caused Jonah to look skyward, but he did not whisper a prayer. He did not repent. If the Lord were sending Jonah to Nineveh, it meant there was time for them to repent, time for them to change. But these were cruel and merciless people; surely, mercy could only reach so far. Even the Lord must have His limits.

The soft dirt gave way to paving stones, and Jonah began to look for a market. From this point, he would have no need for the donkeys, nor were most of his supplies of any value. He would take only enough for a voyage. When he arrived in his own personal exile, he would find a way to survive. Better to be a beggar on the streets of Tarshish than the man who had betrayed his wife's memory.

"Good day, sir," the voice startled Jonah. He turned and saw a shriveled old man with one eye glazed over. The man's fingers were twisted and gnarled.

"Good day to you," Jonah responded, looking quizzically at the strange little man. "Is there a market nearby?" he asked. "I will be traveling by boat and will not need these animals." The odd stranger cocked his head to the right and then to the left looking at both donkeys.

"They're a bit thin," he spoke, pursing his lips, his one good eye squinting. "I might be interested. The name's Baraket. I buy things, sell things, trade things." His finger tips touched as if calculating a price.

Jonah turned from the road into a narrow alley, following Baraket. He almost expected to be jumped by burly men and given a beating for being so gullible. But there was no trap, nor were there any thugs, only a few chickens, a goat, and the smell of wine and urine to greet him.

In a few moments, Jonah received his payment from one of Baraket's twisted hands. Jonah untied from the smaller donkey the two wineskins, two skins filled with water, and a sack containing his remaining food. This should be all he would need. He dropped the newly-acquired money into a small calf-skin pouch at his side. As he passed the donkeys' ropes to Baraket, he thought of how Abidan had placed those same ropes into his own hand.

Jonah stood there frozen, the ropes held by both men. "What am I doing?" The prophet struggled silently within himself. "How can I do this? I was called by the Most High to speak for Him. I was entrusted with His word. My son always wanted to be like me. Can I just run away? What would Abidan think of me?"

"We had a deal! We had a deal!" demanded Baraket, jerking Jonah out of his trance. "Will you cheat an old man?" The words were pitiful from the old man's lips.

"No, no. I was just remembering something," Jonah apologized half-heartedly. He bowed slightly and backed out of the alley. Jonah turned his face toward the sea and walked away slowly.

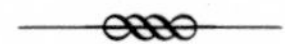

His heart beat hard in his chest, but Jonah continued toward the shoreline. His legs felt heavy. His stomach churned. He was nearing the point of no return.

As far as the eye could see, there were fishermen selling the night's catch, merchants loading and unloading boats, and even a handful of tax collectors, making sure the king got his share. The waves lapped at the shore and sloshed against the wooden hulls of the boats tied to docks or pulled partially onto the beach. A few larger boats were anchored just off shore. Barely anyone paid attention to this runaway prophet. Anonymity was Jonah's fondest wish.

A couple of brawny, deeply-tanned men stood chest-deep in water, hoisting up wooden crates and woven sacks to a slender man on one of the larger boats. Though much smaller than the other two, the thin man showed little sign of strain as the loads were transferred to him. Jonah watched the cargo being loaded as he edged along the shore toward the first man.

He waited until the men stopped to take a short break and then stepped ankle-deep into the gentle waves. "Pardon me, friend," Jonah spoke, hoping this rough-looking man could understand Hebrew. The man turned and studied Jonah and then he spoke something to the prophet in a language Jonah had heard before but could not understand. Jonah shrugged and shook his head from side to side. The man pointed to the slender sailor on deck. Jonah supposed he was indicating that man could help.

Jonah pulled up his robe and waded a bit farther out and shouted above the sounds of the waves splashing against the dark wood of boat. "Pardon me, sir," Jonah spoke. "Do you speak Hebrew?" The lean man caught sight of Jonah with his robe hitched up, trying desperately to keep at least part of his clothing dry, and began to laugh. He called to the other four men aboard the boat to come and see the sight. Two of them broke out into robust laughter; the other two turned back to their tasks, expressing no interest at all.

When the laughter died down, the slim man with coal-black eyes leaned on the rail and spoke in broken Hebrew, "I understand you. What do you want?" Jonah was relieved that he had found someone he could understand, but he still struggled to keep his feet with each wave that pushed against him.

Jonah answered back, "What is your destination? When are you leaving? Can I book passage?"

"We sail for Tarshish," came the sailor's reply. "No passengers. Just cargo." The man waived his arm to let the men know it was time to resume the transfer of cargo from shore to ship. Jonah fumbled for the small leather bag tied at his waist. He held it up, bouncing it in his hand so that the unmistakable sound of coins clinking against other coins could be easily heard. The sailor stopped and raised his hand for the men to cease once more. He looked down at Jonah.

"You want to go to Tarshish? All right. I make room, but it is long voyage. You sleep with cargo. You stay out of way. Deal?"

Jonah nodded his head in the affirmative. The sailor smiled, and Jonah noticed he was missing most of his teeth. He raised his arm and pointed in the direction of the shore. "Wait on shore or help with cargo. We leave soon." He then waved for the cargo to start again as Jonah waded back to shore.

It took nearly two hours to load the cargo and provisions onto the ship for the trip. Jonah watched the two men carry and lift crate after crate with relative ease. He imagined Samson would have had a hard time defeating these two hulking men.

"Tarshish," the word surged back and forth into Jonah's mind with the same rhythm of the waves onto the shore. "The end of the world," he thought. "Can a man go so far that even God cannot find him?" Jonah had no answer for such a foolish question, nor did he know what he would do when he arrived at this destination. He just knew it was as far as he could get from Nineveh. A sharp pain stabbed at his heart; it was also as far as Jonah could get from Abidan.

Jonah stared at the vessel that would assist in his escape. It had become noticeably heavier in the water. He sat on a large rock outcropping, baking in the sun, while the loading continued. He pulled his arm up to use his robe to shade himself. Once he had some slight relief from the sun, Jonah struggled to keep his eyes open. The restless nights had taken their toll.

He thought of Abidan and the boy's heartbreak. He had lost his mother and now he would soon lose his father. He thought of Jethuel who would step in to be a surrogate father to Abidan. Jonah felt a bit of comfort that Jethuel would take that role seriously. Just as the darkness of sleep was about to overtake him, Jonah lurched forward as he was shoved on his back a little too forcefully. He caught himself before losing his balance completely and jerked upright. One of the would-be Samsons towered over him. The man had broad shoulders. His hands were rough and calloused. When the huge man jerked his head toward the boat and began to walk that way, Jonah scrambled to his feet to follow.

When the duo neared the small waves lapping the shoreline, the big man stopped. Jonah pulled up short as well. Without warning, Jonah was scooped up in the man's arms as a father might do to a child. The prophet was startled and let out a gasp. He felt trapped and attempted to roll out of the man's grip. The man strengthened his grip, and the expression on his face showed he was in no mood for Jonah's antics. The tanned hulk turned toward the waves and strode toward the awaiting boat, keeping Jonah mostly dry.

Once they arrived at the vessel, two massive hands reached down from the boat to grasp Jonah under his arms. The pitiful prophet was hoisted head high by his carrier and easily transferred to the well-worn boards on the deck. The man had no more trouble handling Jonah than he did the wooden crates or sacks of wheat.

Soon, Jonah was stood upright where he was face-to-face with the slender sailor. The man stood no taller than Jonah himself. Even so, Jonah felt a little uneasy as the strange man stood there eyeing him and scratching a scraggly, salt-and-pepper beard.

Jonah spoke first, "How much to sail to Tarshish?" The man's smile once again reappeared.

"Does it matter?" the man asked with a matter-of-fact tone. Jonah took off his leather pouch and began to count out coins into the weathered hand of the sailor, slowing his pace as he thought he was nearing what he felt would be a fair price. He kept counting them out, pausing after each coin, knowing that he was being taken advantage of and also knowing that he had no choice. When only a few coins remained in the pouch, the sailor closed his hand around the small mound of coins. "Enough," he spoke.

The sailor then stepped around Jonah to face the two large men who had ferried both cargo and Jonah to the boat. He took four coins from his hand, placing two in the hand of the large man who stood on deck, then leaning down to drop the other two into the hand of the other, who still stood chest-deep in the water. The sailor stepped near the massive man on deck, and they exchanged words that Jonah did not understand. With a nod of his head, the big man slipped overboard. Jonah watched both men stride toward shore where four women wearing colorful scarves waited to greet them. They were undoubtedly prostitutes looking to take some, if not all, of what the men labored half the day to earn. Jonah would typically have felt disgust over the situation, but, somehow, in the moment, he felt sorry for the two brawny men. He remembered the words of Solomon, words that he had quoted many times to the laborers he met: "The labor of the righteous leads to life, but the wages of the wicked to sin."

"I am the captain," the slender sailor interrupted Jonah's thoughts. "We sail now. You can stay on deck or go below." The captain pointed to an opening in the deck as he spoke. "If you fall over," he hesitated, "well, just don't fall over." He turned from Jonah and began to shout orders that the prophet could not understand. The ship came alive with activity as ropes were pulled, and men scampered from one side to the other.

Jonah moved to the railing and stared back at the buildings of Joppa. He was sailing away from Israel, sailing away from all that was familiar, sailing away from everything he knew and loved. For just a moment he thought about jumping overboard and swimming back to shore, but his mind was made up. He was leaving everything behind. There would be no mercy for Nineveh, and Jonah expected he would find none either.

The sailors seemed to settle into a routine on the deck. One man began a song and the other sailors joined in. Jonah did not understand any of it, but it was a happy, upbeat tune. He held to the railing and closed his eyes, trying somehow to get swept up in the song, wanting it to carry him away just as the boat was now doing, but there was no escaping the images he saw. Faces came and went, one morphing into the other: Yael, Abidan, Merari, Jethuel, Chesed and Arieh and Hiram and Urmitu with her haunting emerald eyes, Baraket the merchant, the two hulking workers, the painted prostitutes waving their scarves, and the captain with the nearly toothless smile. As Jonah opened his eyes, he was startled to see that same smile just inches from his face. Jonah jumped back almost losing his balance and tumbling overboard. The captain's thin arm grabbed Jonah and steadied him. "Maybe you go down into hold," he spoke in broken Hebrew. "Hate to lose you so soon to the sea monsters." At this, the captain broke into uproarious laughter.

Jonah turned to make his way down a ladder into the lower part of the boat. As he carefully gripped the rungs and began his descent, he could hear the laughter spreading to all on board. The wayward prophet began to feel deeply sorry for himself. He was fearless before kings but a laughing stock to pagan sailors.

"What more humiliation can I endure?" Jonah whispered to no one in particular.

Once below deck, the voices and the laughter of the sailors above seemed muffled and distant as if they were a thousand miles away. The rhythm of the water against the hull told Jonah they were moving. The light was muted making it difficult to find his way around. The boat jerked, and Jonah grasped a heavy beam to keep from falling. Beneath his feet, he could feel scraping as the boat's keel pushed across what must have been a sand bar. The boat jostled about and came to a full stop once. There was an intensifying of the shouting on deck, then they lurched forward a bit more, and Jonah felt the boat break free. Once again, the sound of water against wood drowned out the voices above.

His eyes adjusted to the dim light below deck. Jonah ducked his head to avoid the timbers and looked for a place to rest. He expected to find hammocks or bedding of some sort, but it seemed that the entire space was full of barrels, crates, and bags. He shifted around a few crates tied together and found an area covered with piles of dirty cloth.

Jonah mumbled under his breath, "What am I doing? What kind of fool?" His words drifted off to nothingness, and Jonah resigned himself to making the best of his situation. He repositioned the pile of cloth and lay down. "What is that smell? Fish? I'll never sleep in this."

Jonah was wrong. The darkness began to wash over him. Wave after wave of exhaustion overtook him. This was it, his break with God and the abandonment of his calling. Life would never be the same.

He forgot the smell as he thought of Yael. He saw her smile as he drifted into sleep. "No," he tried to claw his way back into consciousness, to hold onto the pleasant memory. The vision of Yael's kind face and lovely smile changed. Her dark complexion began to lose its color. Jonah's tears began to roll down his cheeks and onto the stained pile of cloth beneath his head. He felt as if he were drowning in sorrow. Everything went dark as he succumbed to weariness.

6
The Storm

Whether he was awake or still asleep, he could not tell. There was only darkness, a thick, cold, penetrating darkness. Jonah wondered where he was. He remembered boarding a ship. He remembered going below deck. Beyond this, things seemed uncertain. Was he still in the ship? Someplace else? He felt displaced, confined, alone.

The only thing Jonah was really certain about was the darkness and the silence. He strained to hear even the faintest sound, but there was only an eerie quiet. Anxiety caused his heart to race and his breathing to become shallow and labored. He was confused and helpless.

Then he heard it, a voice faint and distant. Jonah could not make it out. He tilted his head, focusing his attention on what was being said. It was just one word repeated over and over. The voice grew closer and louder. He could almost make it out.

In an instant, it became chillingly clear. Only one word - chesed - mercy.

In an instant, the darkness was swallowed up in blinding light. Jonah squeezed his eyes tightly against the radiance. Slowly, he blinked and began to look into the light. He shielded his eyes and squinted to see the blurry images moving only an arm's length away - faces without bodies parading before him, fading in and out of focus. The images of men, women and children appeared and disappeared in rapid succession. With each face Jonah heard loudly and, now, clearly the word "mercy." Like a visual drumbeat, the faces came one after another, some weeping and some somber but with eyes pleading and brimming with tears. Ashes fell on their heads like a heavy winter snowfall.

Jonah wondered at each face. Though he did not know their names, he began to pity them. How many had passed? Dozens? Hundreds? How many tears had he seen? Why were they so dejected and sad?

Jonah joined them in their sorrow, though he did not know them nor the cause for their distress. An ocean of sympathy consumed him. But why? Why had these faces come to him? He did not know who they were or where they were. He did not know the great disaster that brought them to such a low and wretched state.

As he witnessed the last of the faces in the piteous parade pass, Jonah saw a throne with a man seated upon it. Without taking a step, he felt himself drawing closer.

The man upon the throne had set aside his crown. He was bent as if carrying a massive burden on his shoulders. From his hair, ashes fell onto his body. His cheeks black where ash had mixed with tears. No gold rings adorned his fingers, nor was there a golden chain around his neck. He wore no fine robe, only simple, coarse sackcloth that hung loosely on him.

Jonah was just two paces from him as the king lifted his face and looked into the prophet's eyes. "Mercy," he pleaded in a pitiful, shaky voice. "Mercy. Have mercy."

As the plea echoed in Jonah's mind, everything faded into darkness as if a heavy curtain were falling from the sky. The darkness was empty, yet felt full of dread and sorrow. At that moment, Jonah's whole world began to shake and roll. As he was jostled about in the inky darkness, Jonah began to feel cold and wet.

With the world reeling chaotically around him, Jonah still slept.

As the wayward prophet slept below the deck, the seas on which the small cargo ship sailed had turned from a soft blue carpet rising and falling in perfect rhythm to a churning cauldron raging and heaving like a man possessed. The boat lifted high in the water only to come crashing down, sending swells of water over the bow and across the deck. Winds blasted the vessel, seeming to come from every direction at once.

The rudder could not be held steady. The boat was a helpless victim in a vicious storm. The captain shouted commands over the howling winds, but it was all the sailors could do to keep from being swept over the side. Wave after wave pounded the boat. Every attempt to secure the hull with ropes was thwarted by the relentless surge of wind and water.

"We can't keep this up, sir. We're taking on a lot of water," one of the crew shouted above the tumult. The slender captain rallied his strength and took his stand as the deck rolled beneath his feet.

"Cargo overboard," he barked. "We must lighten the ship if we are to survive!" He joined the small crew in hauling their precious cargo up and tossing it over in a seemingly vain attempt to keep the waterlogged vessel afloat. It mattered very little what each crate or sack contained. The men fought to survive a storm unlike anything they had ever seen before.

The captain half climbed and half fell into the cargo hold. Standing in seawater up to his knees, he began to pass one soggy sack after another when he caught sight of his one and only passenger. The man appeared almost dead. His body was half submerged in the water that sloshed around him.

Grabbing an overhead beam, the captain took uncertain steps toward the motionless body. He kicked at him to determine if he were alive or dead. Whether it was the force of the kick or a sudden spray of water that suddenly sprang from the compromised hull, Jonah woke startled and shaking, immediately comprehending the chaos was not only in his dream.

"How can you sleep?" the captain screamed. "Get up. All this has to go overboard."

Jonah was utterly disoriented. Nothing made sense.

The captain continued to scream at Jonah, "Can you pray? If you can do nothing else, pray! Ask your god to help us. Pray to your god. Maybe he will hear you. Maybe he will save us."

Jonah did not pray. He splashed through the water up to his thighs and scrambled up the ladder between sacks being tossed onto deck. The prophet attempted to get to his feet but found himself thrown this way and that. He surrendered to crawling, trying to find something solid of which he could take hold. He tasted the seawater as it ran down his hair and into his half-open mouth.

All around him was nothing but madness. Wind and water seemed to fight one another, and the boat was caught up in their spat. The faces of hardened seamen showed flashes of fear as lightning streaked across the sky. Jonah closed his eyes, hoping that all this might go away, but even with eyes shut tightly, he knew the terrifying sight would be there once he dared peek.

The pitching and creaking of the boat caused Jonah to tighten his grip on the slippery railing. With eyes squeezed shut, Jonah could hear the wind whipping through what remained of the sails and the words of the men in the midst of the crashing of titanic waves onto the deck. Although he could not understand what they were saying, their intent was plain. Each man prayed as he tossed cargo overboard or clung to some small piece of the boat.

One man chanted with a tune eerily similar to a hymn Jonah had taught Abidan. He tried to remember how it went. "Answer me when I call to you, my righteous God. Give me relief from my distress; have mercy on me and hear my prayer." With eyes closed, Jonah let the tune play in his mind, yet it was more a comforting memory than an attempt at prayer.

"Asleep again, are you?" screamed the captain above the shrieking wind. Jonah threw open his eyes to see the slender captain's black eyes only inches from his own. He seemed somehow impervious to the storm. No matter which way the boat pitched, this man of the sea kept his feet. The captain took hold of Jonah's beard and stared at him through squinting eyes. "What are you doing?"

he screamed to be heard over the howling wind. "You are not praying, man? My men call out in fear to Yamm, to Baal, to Astarte, to whatever god or goddess they can think of, but you hold fast to the railing and utter not a single word to your god."

A heavy wave pounded the ship only momentarily distracting the captain. He resumed his tirade, "Has your god abandoned you? Have you abandoned your god? Do you have no fear of dying?" His face fell suddenly still. "Who *are* you? Did you bring this..." the captain struggled to find words to describe a storm the likes of which even he had never seen.

With surprising strength, the captain pulled Jonah by his beard as Jonah struggled to gain his feet and follow. He led the pathetic prophet to the main mast and dislodged one green sailor who had wrapped both arms and legs around the mast in a desperate attempt not to be washed overboard. When the captain released his beard, Jonah took hold of the mast for support. He wanted to pray, to confess, to seek mercy. He did not.

7

THE LOTS

All the cargo having been thrown overboard, the captain stood facing the praying sailors and a runaway prophet. He shouted above the howl and spray, "Never have I seen a storm like this. We have lost our goods. There is to be no profit in this voyage, and we will be fortunate to survive with our lives. It must be that a god is angry with one of us and will destroy us all if he is not satisfied. So…who is it? Who is guilty? Let him speak now to save the lives of the rest!"

Nothing was heard but the storm pounding against the boat that seemed so fragile on the raging waves that it could break apart at any moment. "Speak!" shouted the captain. "Show some courage and confess your affront."

Jonah did not understand the seaman's words, but he knew full well what he was asking. As the captain's eyes darted from man to man, Jonah looked down. He felt his eyes would betray him. When he dared to look up again, he saw the captain's thin face just inches from his own.

In broken Hebrew the man spoke, "Is it you? Are you the guilty one? Did your god send the storm? Does he try to kill you because he is angry? Can you not speak?" Jonah did not answer but knew his face betrayed his guilt.

A nearby sailor, hearing the captain's words, released his grip on a side rail and staggered toward Jonah and the captain. He pulled a pouch from his leather belt and held it out before them. His face was painted with desperation. "Let us cast lots to determine which of us has offended the gods and brought this calamity on us all."

The captain took the pouch and emptied the sheep knuckles into his palm. He counted out eight and pocketed the other two. Seven of those that went back into the pouch were bleached white, but the other was a brownish color. The captain's lips moved in silent prayer as he shook the pouch. He then went from man to man who reached in and pulled out one of the bones. Each man closed his hand around the unwelcomed prize until all the others had chosen his lot. The captain reached his thin, weathered hand in the pouch to remove the final piece of bone. The sailors and Jonah stared at their closed hands, and then one by one they shifted their gaze to the captain.

With a simple gesture, the ship's captain opened his palm to reveal his lot. Each sailor followed his example. Through eyes blinking against the constant spray of seawater, Jonah saw each of the sheep knuckles held in the seamen's palms, then he noted that all eyes were focused on his own still-closed hand. The runaway prophet looked down as his fingers almost involuntarily fell open.

There in his palm was a bone much darker in color than all the others; the difference was obvious. Jonah let it roll from his hand onto the boat's deck where a wash of seawater carried it to the bare feet of the captain.

There was no more hiding. The men were convinced that Jonah was the guilty party, and this ungodly storm was his god's vengeance upon him. They begin to pepper him with questions, though honestly, Jonah could not understand much of what the sailors were saying. The captain seemed to be translating rapid-fire the queries of his shipmates. "What kind of work do you do? Where do you come from? What is your country? Who are your people?" He paused, then, "Confess! Are you responsible for all of this?"

His tears mixing with the sea spray, Jonah held to the mast and poured out his confession while the captain shouted the translation as best he could.

"I am a Hebrew of Israel," Jonah began. "I worship the Lord who is God of heaven. It is He who made the sea as well as the dry land. He is the Creator. I am…" Jonah's voice broke. He breathed in deeply and completed his sentence, "I am His prophet. He called me to go and preach, but I could not - I would not go. I just want to get away from everything."

As Jonah spoke, the sailors' eyes grew wide. They were fearful in the face of the storm's assault, but now their fear was compounded by the fact that they had a prophet on board who had turned his back on his god. "What have you done to us?" screamed the captain. As if joining in the incredulity, the rain became torrential, and the winds churned the sea even more.

One of the sailors lost his grip and began to slide across the slanted deck, slamming into the mast onto which Jonah clung for his life. Wincing in pain, the man looked up at Jonah with pleading eyes. Though he could not understand what the man was saying, it was plain to Jonah that the injured man was pleading for something to be done to calm the raging sea.

"This is your doing," the captain shouted at Jonah. A vicious wall of water pounded the scrawny man causing him to fall hard on the deck. As he scrambled to his feet, the captain looked intently into Jonah's eyes, "Tell us what we must do. Do you want us all to die?"

Jonah had abandoned his son, his mission, and his God. He had sought to run so far that the God of Abraham, Isaac, and Jacob could not reach him. He knew it was foolishness, but his wounded heart would not allow him to continue his journey to Nineveh. And now, as he saw the frightened faces of the seamen desperately clinging to life and praying desperate prayers to their false gods, Jonah realized he had forfeited his own life. He was lost in a sea of despair, but these men, though pagans, did not need to be swept away with him in the Lord's judgment.

Perhaps he should just leap overboard and end it all. He did not know if God would relent, but he knew the Lord was merciful even to pagans. It was this understanding of God's mercy that had put Jonah at the center of the storm.

He knew he could not survive if he took the few short steps to the vessel's rails and threw himself overboard. The thought of taking his own life chilled him far more than the frigid seawater that soaked his robes. Jonah had to admit to himself that fear kept him from letting go of the mast and bringing an end to his now miserable life. In the not too distant past, men had thought him brave to stand before a king and proclaim God's truth, but holding to the main mast as the boat tossed in the waves, Jonah was not standing for truth or standing for God. He was running from him.

"Running from God," he thought. "What complete madness! I deserve to die, to sink to the darkest depths of the sea, but I cannot."

It was not courage that caused Jonah to speak; he spoke out of utter hopelessness. "Pick me up," he finally spoke to the captain. "This is all my doing, all my fault. I have angered my God by turning my back on Him. Pick me up and throw me into the sea. Do this, and the seas will become calm. Let this end now." The Lord had not told Jonah this, but the fallen prophet knew what kind of God he once worshiped and revered. He knew in the depths of his heart Israel's God was merciful.

Having confessed, Jonah fully expected the terrified sailors to rush him at once, offer a quick prayer to whatever deity or deities they worshiped, and then he would be hastily tossed over the side into the cold, churning caldron. Jonah waited, but none of them moved for what seemed an eternity.

Jonah looked from man to man, then turned his gaze again to the captain. The old seaman's dark eyes stared intently at the pitiful prophet clinging to the mast. In an instant, the captain's demeanor change. A look of steely determination filled his face, and his body became erect. His features seemed fuller and stronger as he pointed his finger at each man, giving commands:

"Unstrap the oars, men. We will not taste death this day." He steadied himself. "Our ship is battered but not sunk. She holds, men, she holds, and she will hold. To the oars! We'll make for shore. Perhaps, if we show this god of sea and storm that we mean to take his prophet back, he will show us mercy. Row, men, row! Put your backs in it. To the oars! To the oars!"

The captain's boldness filled the men with courage. They leapt to the task, untying oars and securing them in the sockets. Each man in position, the captain took up his cadence, "Row, row, row." And they rowed, arms and backs straining to pull the vessel free of the raging waves around them. They lost their balance often but held fast to the oars.

Jonah observed their effort at self-preservation with wonder. How these men cherished their lives; they likely had wives and children to support. They wanted to come home to their families, to die not in a storm but of old age with the sounds of squealing grandchildren filtering in through an open window. Yes, they were idolaters, but they were also human. For the first time Jonah saw them not merely as filthy pagans but as men.

One sailor pulling at the oars suddenly jerked backwards violently. The extreme tension on his oar had caused it to snap. His head hit hard against the deck, and his body went limp at the impact. The other sailors continued pulling on their oars while the injured man rocked side to side with the motion of the ship's deck. Jonah considered letting go of the mast to help, but then his eyes were drawn to a wall of dark green and gray coming rapidly toward the ship's bow. The captain was oblivious as he stood on the tilted deck hollering encouragement at his brave men. Only Jonah saw it coming, but any warning he might have offered could not have helped. Surely, this was the final outpouring of God's wrath that would swallow them all. He thought of Yael and of Abidan…

The wave hit.

The bow began to rise at an awful pitch, sending the captain and four sailors tumbling toward the stern. Each grabbed at anything he could. The water slammed the small vessel with unimaginable ferocity. Everything tilted sharply starboard as the men let go of the oars, doing all they could to simply hold on for their lives.

Jonah felt gravity tugging him toward the cold, dark water. What the men would not do, God would do himself, taking all aboard into the churning sea. "The God of all mercy," Jonah thought, "has come to the end of His patience."

Having surrendered himself to the thought, Jonah almost let go of the mast to hasten his fate. Amazingly, the ship righted itself. Jonah felt his feet settle on the wood deck once more. The sea was still raging, but the boat had managed to survive. Looking at his surroundings, Jonah counted the sailors. All were present. The captain held to a railing with one arm and held the helpless, unconscious sailor with the other. One word played over and over in Jonah's mind, "Chesed. Mercy."

As the sailors began to catch their breath, Jonah heard the strangest thing. He could not make out all of what they were saying, but interspersed among the foreign words, he caught the name "Yahweh." They were calling out to the Lord. These pagan men who from the storm's onset had prayed to their gods were now beseeching the Lord for His favor.

Jonah scanned the deck, and his eyes locked with the captain's. His jaw was set in the same look of determination that Jonah had seen earlier when the captain had made the decision to row back to land. In light of what they had endured, he had chosen another course of action.

"Prophet," the captain said, "we will do as you say and cast you overboard. May the Lord have mercy on us. I, for one, am convinced that this God of yours is Lord of both land and sea. The blast of his nostrils stirs the deep and causes the sea to show its fury. We are tossed about like a child's toy, yet He has spared our lives somehow," he paused. "Perhaps, He will show the same mercy to you."

The captain shifted the unconscious man to another sailor then made his way to Jonah. Two others came after him. Jonah had always hoped he would die in the arms of his wife and with the touch of his son. Today, the last human touch he would feel would be the calloused hands and sea-soaked arms of the men who plunged him to his death. Jonah released the mast and walked the few steps to the side railing. The captain turned his eyes upward and prayed, "Please, Lord, do not let us die for taking this man's life. Do not hold us accountable for killing an innocent man, for You, Lord, have done as you pleased."

The captain motioned for the two sailors to take hold of Jonah under the arms while he took Jonah's feet. They lifted him up. Jonah closed his eyes, not wanting to see the pained look on the captain's face.

Jonah felt himself swing backward toward the mast then forward. Suddenly the arms that had held him were gone. He was suspended for only a moment in mid air. The sailors who watched the event would later tell their children that it was not that the prophet fell into the water but that the waves rose up to consume him. Jonah did not bob on the surface. One moment he was there, and the next moment he was gone.

As Jonah disappeared under the surface, the raging wind above immediately became a gentle breeze, and sea ceased its fury and slowed to a calm. The dark clouds that had kept them in perpetual night parted, and the sun beat down upon the faces of the sailors on board the battered ship.

The men on the ship's deck stared at each other, mouths open. The captain cocked his head and lifted an eye to the cloudless sky he had truly never expected to see again. He shifted his gaze to his battered crew and saw that even the hardest of them smiled at their good fortune. "A sacrifice to the Lord of heaven and earth, the God of Jonah," he said in a firm but reverent tone as the deck gently rocked beneath their feet. Each man fumbled in the pouches tied at his waist or scampered below to scavenge for anything of value that might remain.

They gathered the miscellaneous items: two silver coins, a piece of polished metal used as a mirror, a short sword, a handful of dates, locks of hair from three of the men, including the one who had been knocked unconscious during the storm. That man now leaned against the center mast with a makeshift bandage wrapped around his head.

The men stood in a half circle near the bow of the ship, and in his own language, each made a vow to honor the Lord as his God and one by one tossed the semi-precious item he held into the gently rolling waves. They stood watching silently the calm sea, not knowing what to expect if anything at all.

The captain finally broke their solemn silence, "Men, let's go home."

8
THE FISH

What Jonah expected would be an immediate plunge into the dark waves became like a long, frightening fall. He had intended to face his drowning death calmly and bravely, perhaps to recapture a small bit of the dignity he had shown in the king's court, but he found himself flailing around, his arms and legs in desperate motion as if somehow he could grab the wind and avoid the sea's grasp. He could not.

His body landed hard, and Jonah gasped, inhaling a mouthful of salty water. He closed his mouth and tried to right himself in the water. He looked for the boat, for the sky, for anything. Up and down had lost all meaning as his body was tossed in the churning waters. He tried to calm himself thinking he might then float to the surface, but Jonah only felt as if he were sinking deeper. He kicked his legs, and his arms reached out seeking to be free from his watery captivity, but the sea seemed to go on infinitely in every direction.

Panic began to set in. Jonah's mind franticly tried to think of any way out of his situation. His lungs began to burn. They begged for one breath of air, but his mind told him to keep his mouth closed and hold on just a little longer.

It felt like thousands of icy fingers were taking hold of his body and pulling him ever downward. He struggled but soon became all the more entangled in seaweed. He thrashed about trying to free himself. The desperation of his movements mirrored the frantic desperation of Jonah's lungs. This was it. The rebellion was ending. The fleeing prophet was undone by his own foolish plan of escape.

He calmed himself and closed his eyes. He wanted his last thoughts to be of Yael, of Abidon, of love and laughter. The faces came and went in this mind. He saw images of King Jeroboam, of Merari and Jethuel, of the sailors fighting against the raging storm. The images faded into blackness. Jonah went limp. He prepared to meet the fate he knew that he deserved, and then he remembered emerald eyes, Urmitu's eyes. Was that her voice he heard? "Chesed…chesed…mercy…"

The word that once caused Jonah to turn his back on the Lord's calling now seemed like a sweet melody. Was there any mercy for him or was there only overwhelming regret and a watery grave? "Mercy" - the word continued to tumble through Jonah's mind. It turned from a memory to a prayer, and Jonah realized that it was the first time he had prayed in many, many days. "Lord, have mercy on me, a poor wayward prophet."

Jonah would die. He would stand before the Lord whom He had rejected and hope for the one thing he refused to show the people of Nineveh, mercy. He opened his mouth to draw in the sea, then suddenly his dark world became pitch black. Jonah's eyes were wide, but he saw nothing. His surroundings had suddenly changed. Jonah was contained on all sides by something soft, wet, smelly. He pushed against the confining space. It pressed tightly in on Jonah forcing the little oxygen left in his lungs through his mouth, and then he inhaled expecting his lungs to fill with water, yet somehow he drew in air.

9
The Prayer

There was little room to move. It was dark and cold and slimy and hard to breathe. Jonah's anxiety rose as he wondered what had become of him. He coughed and nearly gagged before regaining his composure.

He tried to move his hands in the confined space, attempting to discover some clue as to where he was and what had happened to him. He felt something around him, like wet leather, soft but strong. He moved his fingers a few inches and felt what seemed to be a pole. Several inches over, he felt another. With more exploration, he found that these poles curved as they went upward and were spaced closely together with the wet leather between them and covering them.

He tried to calm himself and listen intently to his surroundings. He recognized the sound; it was all too familiar. It was the sound of water against the boat's hull. How was that possible? He vividly remembered the events of the past few hours: the storm's ceaseless fury, the desperation of the sailors, and his short passage from the deck of the ship to the dark waters. Was he somehow still on board the boat? Had the storm itself been yet another nightmare?

But no, there was another sound, a steady thumping sound. Drums? Oars? His mind raced to make sense of this puzzle.

An overwhelming sense of panic began to well up within Jonah. He struggled against his confinement to no avail. After minutes of fruitless fighting, he once again resolved to figure out what was going on. He felt his firm but slimy surroundings, yet, again, he noted the smell of something rotten, listened to the rhythmic thumping somewhere just beyond his reach, and sensed a movement as if he were inside something alive.

"Something alive. Alive? No!" his mind reeled, and then it all became clear. "A fish! Could it be? Have I been eaten by some great fish?"

Jonah pounded on the wet surface around him. He screamed. He tried to move himself forward to the fish's mouth but was unsure as to whether he was facing the mouth or tail. He became still. Again, he tried to calm himself trying to breath slowly. "Why am I not dead?" he thought, his mind racing. "Why is the Lord preserving me? What kind of fool am I to think I could somehow run from the Almighty? He will yet have His way." Jonah closed his eyes and wept bitter tears for all he had lost.

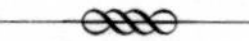

How long had he been here? Minutes? Hours? Days? Was he still alive? Was he dead? Was this Sheol?

Jonah struggled to move. His entire right side was sore and achy. He repositioned himself in the slime. His pain, along with a nagging hunger and insatiable thirst, made it perfectly clear to Jonah that he was still among the living. Somehow, in the belly of this fish, Jonah had fallen into a deep, dreamless sleep. Having awakened, he found the air was thick and dank. Jonah struggled to catch each breath. He was still alive, though for how much longer he could not know. Jonah wondered if this was God's final judgment on an unfaithful servant or if this might be His way of showing mercy. As he ran his fingers along the walls of this living tomb, his only company was the painful memories and deep regrets that were now his constant companions.

How long had it been since Jonah had opened his heart to God? How long since he had prayed, really, from the depths of his soul?

He had run from God's call for fear of His showing mercy to the Ninevites. In his present misery, Jonah was desirous of that very mercy. Could this confinement be God's answer?

Jonah looked up, or what he believed to be up, and poured out the desperation in his heart.

"Lord, God, I am in deep distress. I was nearly dead in the sea, and you somehow saved me. You heard my cry, and You answered me. I ran from You, but You pursued me. You cast me into the sea and caused the waters to pull me down. I was wrapped in seaweed for my grave clothes. I tried to run far from You as far as a man can run, but found myself alone in the depths and perhaps even out of Your reach. I was as good as dead and may yet succumb, but for now You have rescued me. Here in this great fish, I still have some small glimmer of hope that I may still be delivered by Your hand and once more go up to Jerusalem to be in Your presence.

"I have seen the worthless idols of men and heard the prayers of the sailors to their false gods. They prayed, but their gods could not answer them. You somehow loved them and spared them even though they did not honor You. My life has not shown You the honor that is due Your holy name, but I will honor You! I will shout grateful praise to You. I will offer sacrifices to You. I vow it to You this day; deliver me and I will serve You faithfully."

Jonah listened. Would he once more hear the word of the Lord? Would God speak mercy or judgment? All was quiet, disturbingly so. Fear began to creep into Jonah's heart. Had the Lord abandoned him at last?

As he waited, the fear became a consuming terror, and no matter what awaited him in the waters, Jonah knew he had to free himself. He kicked hard against the fish's ribs, clawed at the slick, wet walls that imprisoned him, but there was no change. Jonah gulped at the thin air and knew he could not continue much longer before exhaustion set in. As he slowed to take a deep breath and try again, he heard what he could only compare to a deep moan, and then felt a hard bump.

The slick walls around Jonah began to move erratically, and Jonah felt the fish start to convulse. The jerking flesh pressed in on Jonah, pushing hard against his legs. The pain of his legs being pressed together brought a muffled scream from his throat. He tried hard to relax and to still himself, not knowing what would happen next. The spasms pressed Jonah forward, freeing his legs but bending his neck at an awkward angle. At that moment, Jonah saw it, something he had not seen in days. It was light, brilliant, almost blinding. Jonah pulled an arm free and reached for the light just as he felt the spasms pushing him toward it.

Jonah slid out of the fish's mouth into the surf. He was too weak to swim. Was he set free from his imprisonment only to drown? As he tumbled and twisted with the waves, his grasping hands found sand. Working his feet downward, he gained enough strength to push upward. Air! Jonah took huge gulps.

A wave caught him and pushed him forward into shallow water. His fingers dug into the sand as he crawled, slowly pulling himself forward, toward an outcropping of rocks, gulping deep breaths of fresh air. His hands were pale and covered in a slimy film; his robe was ripped and tattered. Jonah grasped one of the rocks and held tightly to it.

Pulling himself forward toward the beach, he was shaky and weak. Jonah tried to stand but found he simply could not. He let the waves push him forward into ever shallower water until he finally collapsed in the sand.

He was free. Free...the word repeated in his head, though he could barely believe it. In spite of all that happened, God had delivered him.

Jonah raised his head and looked beyond the waves, hoping to see the great fish that had been both his prison and his salvation. All he saw was a pinkish gray form followed by a huge splash. It lasted only a moment, and then it was gone.

The weary prophet lay in the wet sand until his breathing calmed. He felt the pangs of hunger and a desperate thirst, but he did not have the strength to move.

Jonah rolled over onto his back and watched the clouds drift high above him. Could this be real? Was he truly given a second chance? "Salvation comes from the Lord," he said, his voice rasping. "Salvation truly comes from the Lord."

The intense warmth of the sun on Jonah's bleached white skin lessened as clouds gathered. A gentle rain began to fall, and Jonah opened his mouth. He licked his chapped lips with the heaven sent moisture. He closed his eyes to pray, but instead the sound of seagulls and breakers lulled him to sleep.

10
The New Call

Jonah stood on shaky legs, thirsty and hungry, but he was alive. He leaned heavily upon the rocks and reflected on the past few days. He could still feel how the wind had stung at his face as he stood in defiance of the Lord. He thought of his decision to turn his back on the call to go to Nineveh, of how he had almost cost the sailors their lives, and of his dark captivity inside the fish.

Slowly, Jonah took feeble steps back toward the sea. He stopped for a moment to survey the water for any sign of the great fish. Satisfied there was no danger, he submerged himself up to his waist and began to wash away the remnants of the fish's stomach from his body. The water was warm. He scooped handfuls onto his hair and scrubbed at his face. His skin was very pale and a putrid smell clung to him.

Mustering all the strength he could, Jonah walked on tender, bare feet a short way up the beach to a small growth of trees which had become twisted over the years by constant winds. He sat down with his back against the rough bark. Home. He wanted to go home. He wanted to place his hands on Abidan's shoulders and look into his eyes. He wanted to sleep and to forget everything that had happened.

A dark cloud blocked the sun's rays, and a cool breeze on Jonah's face caused him to sigh with contentment. "Jonah," came that familiar voice. Jonah's heart skipped a beat. There it was. He took deep breaths, steadying himself for whatever God would speak, whether mercy or judgment. With a deep gulp the reluctant prophet answered, "I am here, Lord."

"Jonah, get up," came the Lord's gentle but firm voice. Jonah scrambled to his feet and stepped away from the trees. His head was bowed. He was a beaten man. He had defied God and lost. He had run from God, but there was no escape from the Lord's reach.

"Go to Nineveh." Jonah could feel his muscles tense. He thought of objecting, of stating all the reasons why the Ninevites deserved swift and certain justice. He wanted to shout Yael's name, to ask God if He remembered how she died or even if He cared, but Jonah did not say a word as the clouds parted and the sun again beat down on his face.

He looked toward the calm sea and remembered how it had churned with His fury. To defy God a second time would surely be worse than the first. He had been shown mercy. He would go. He would go to that great and wicked city. When he arrived, he would tell them God's judgment was coming, and then he would watch the city burn. He turned his back on the sea and began his long journey to Nineveh.

Jonah made his way toward a grove of olive trees, hoping to find water. His steps were still unsteady but determined. Just ahead he heard voices, and Jonah moved toward them. He reached a stone wall, sat down, and then attempted to move his legs over to the other side. Instead, he found himself falling over the wall. As he hit the ground, Jonah groaned loudly, causing the voices to stop and a man and boy to peek around the trees toward the sound.

Jonah moved quickly to recover his composure. He looked up into a weathered and tanned face. The man had deep brown eyes visible under the hood of his cloak. His long, thick beard was streaked with gray. He spoke to Jonah with an almost comical, high-pitched voice, "Are you hurt? Can you stand?"

"I think so," Jonah replied weakly. The man reached under Jonah's arm and helped him to stand. Jonah leaned heavily on the fence. "May I have some water?" he spoke through dry lips.

"Bildad, go fetch water. Stop staring. Go quickly, boy." The youth darted away into the stand of olive trees as the older man kept his attention on Jonah. "What happened to you, sir?" he asked as he looked at Jonah's unearthly appearance.

A small, weak smile curled the corner of Jonah's mouth. "Happened? I'm not sure anyone would believe me. I was on a ship…there was storm…I was tossed into the water…," Jonah did not finish. The man would not believe he had survived being eaten by a fish, and Jonah certainly did not want to confess that he was a prophet running from God.

"Tossed overboard!" the man responded, seemingly satisfied with Jonah's answer. Jonah noted that the man spoke Hebrew flawlessly. "Where are you from?" the kind stranger asked.

"Gath-hepher. My father was Amittai." Jonah almost let it slip that he was a prophet. It was who he was. It was his calling. He was filled with shame at the thought that he had run from God. Perhaps, confessing it to this stranger would lessen the burden. Surely, he would understand how Jonah would reject a call to go to Nineveh! When had the Lord ever asked any prophet to do such a thing? To preach the destruction of a wicked city from Israel was one thing; to stand in that city's streets to proclaim the Lord's judgment was another. What if they did what the Jews had done so many times before and turned from their sins?

These thoughts were interrupted when the boy came clear of the trees and skidded to a stop. "Father," he shouted as he handed his father a well-worn skin and stepped back, a little wary of the stranger on the wall. The father quickly pulled out the plug and handed the skin to Jonah. The thirsty prophet opened his mouth and drank deeply of the fresh, clear water. Twice he coughed and gagged, trying to drink too much at once. The older man put his hand on Jonah's shoulder and encouraged him to take it slowly.

When Jonah had drunk his fill, the man helped him to his feet and led him through the olive grove to a modest clay brick house. He pushed back the heavy woven blanket that covered the entrance, revealing a sparse interior. The boy ran ahead of them and quickly returned with a few worn pillows. He placed them in a corner near an open window. Jonah was led to the pillows and laid gently on them. "Rest," the man told him. "I will go fetch some food."

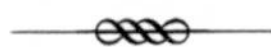

Jonah woke to the sound of singing and rose carefully from his bed. He thought it was strange that he didn't remember going to bed. He was fully dressed, as if for a journey including the sandals on his feet. He reflected on the peculiar circumstances but was soon distracted by the beautiful melodies of a woman's voice. How many times had he heard that voice, and how many times had it had made him melt inside? Yael's singing could cause the larks to cease their songs and listen.

He threw back the yellow and red covering over the window and peered out. There she was, draping wet laundry on the fence to dry. She was wearing the same ornate robe she had worn in their wedding ceremony. Again, Jonah thought it was strange, but he could not remove his eyes from the beauty of her form nor could he tear himself away from the splendor of her voice. His love for her had never felt stronger than at that moment.

As Jonah gazed at his wife going about her daily chores, he suddenly noticed a red stain beginning to form across her back. It grew larger with each passing moment, but she did not seem to notice. She continued her song and her task. Jonah swallowed hard and tore himself away from the window and swiftly moved through the doorway. He ran to her, but the sand gave way beneath his feet. He struggled forward, calling her name, but no sound came from his mouth. He could only hear the song she sang, a song about God's mercy toward those who turn to Him.

The short distance between them narrowed with an agonizing slowness, but Jonah was determined to reach his wife. Her robe, once a brilliant white, was now saturated with a thick, crimson wetness. He did not want it to be true, but he knew that it was. He was so close he could almost touch her. He reached out to her, the tips of his fingers touching her shoulder. He drew back his hand almost immediately and gazed in horror at the blood on his fingertips.

"Yael," he spoke, and this time the word came out. She turned, but slowly, as if time itself were winding down. He simply wanted to see her face, but he was certain that it would be pale, as the blood and the life seeped from her body. What he saw startled him. This was not Yael. He looked into the emerald green eyes of Urmitu. Softly, she spoke, "Chesed…mercy…"

He woke up screaming, "No! No! No!" His head jerked quickly from side to side as if to erase all that he had just experienced. The room was dark except for the flickering flame from a clay lamp on the far wall. The smell of burning olive oil and the feel of the worn pillows under him were an instant reminder of where he was and all that had transpired to get him to this place.

Bildad came running quickly from outside, and his father followed closely behind him. The boy stayed a safe distance away, but the man came to Jonah and knelt in front of him.

"I am Eliam," spoke the homeowner, smiling at him and pushing back his hood. Jonah simply stared at the man unable to grasp what was real. As he strained to focus, he remembered the tanned skin, the deep brown eyes, the thick and graying beard. His eyes, however, fixed on a scar beginning under Eliam's hairline and running down the left side of his face. Jonah wondered why he had not noticed it before. He saw the man's lips moving, but it took a few moments for the words to penetrate the thick fog of sleep. "Can you hear me? Are you hungry? Are you hurting?"

"Eliam..." the word was as much a question as a statement. "Where am I?"

Eliam answered quietly, "You are in the olive groves of my master, Asu. Bildad and I tend the trees." Jonah's expression still showed confusion, so Eliam continued, "We are near Tartus."

Jonah sat up. "Tartus?" He rubbed his forehead as if trying to wipe away his confusion. He was a long way from Joppa.

Jonah, suddenly alert, asked, "The day…what day is it?"

Eliam answered, "It is Yom Rishon. Do not worry. You have only slept a few hours. Food is ready. Can you eat?"

Jonah did a quick calculation. He whispered to himself, "Three days. I was in the fish for three days." He struggled to get up from the pillows.

Bildad rushed to Jonah's side and helped to lift him. Jonah could remember when Abidan was his age. All three made their way out the door and to a large shade tree where Bildad helped Jonah sit with his back against the trunk for support. The three men sat crossed-legged on the ground. A gentle breeze made the coming evening pleasant. Eliam turned his eyes upward and held his palms open, "Lord, God of my fathers, thank You for Your blessings, and for this man whom You have sent into our care."

The men ate in silence, a meal of roasted goat and bread along with some greens. Jonah ate slowly. His hands shook, but he wasn't sure if it was because of his hunger, the three days he spent in the fish's belly, or his dream of Yael. He was full far sooner than he wished, and he knew the hunger would return again before morning.

Eliam broke the silence, "You are not a sailor." It was said as a statement, but Eliam's eyes indicated it was also a question.

"No," replied Jonah.

"So, where are you from?" continued the man.

Jonah answered, "Gath-hepher. Do you know it?"

Eliam's smile appeared once more, "Oh, yes. I am from Rimmon. My father was Dan." His voice fell, "…but that was a long time ago."

Jonah had no desire to share why he had ended up in Tartus. He figured the best way to avoid it was to encourage Eliam to share about his life. He pushed, "So why are you here tending another man's olive grove?"

Eliam looked at his son. The smile disappeared from his face. "When I was young, I was full of ambition. My flocks grew large, and my dates and olive crops produced bountifully. I became one of the wealthiest men around, but I was…," he hesitated and his gaze dropped, "I was greedy. I tried to buy even more land. I hired many laborers to keep me from going into the fields and countryside. I spent my days in town drinking and gambling. I accumulated many debts, debts I could not pay. Some men took their pound of flesh for my debts," Eliam touched the scar on his face, "but I guess I ended up owing the wrong man too much. I am here with my son to work off the debt. Perhaps, my son will see freedom, but it is certain I will not."

Before Jonah could ask another question to keep the focus off himself, Eliam inquired, "Before you were washed overboard, where were you going?"

Jonah spoke without looking up, knowing his face might reveal more than he wanted to, and said, "Tarshish."

Eliam sat up, as did his son. Jonah's attempt to make his destination seem routine had not worked. "Tarshish! That is a long way off," said Eliam. "What business did you have there?"

"I was running away." Jonah was not sure why he had said this out loud. He knew those words could not be left hanging in the air. He was right.

The boy leaned in, hoping to hear more, but Jonah did not know what more he could or should say. How could he tell a fellow Jew that he was a prophet who had turned his back on God? Beyond that, how could he reveal that God had sent him to Nineveh?

"You were running from what?" the boy nearly squealed. Eliam put his hand on his son's shoulder and squeezed, causing Bildad to wince but instantly curbing the boy's enthusiasm. Then, Eliam turned his face to Jonah. His expression showed that he, too, was very interested in hearing the answer to his son's question.

The sun was dropping behind the olive trees, and the long shadows would soon be replaced by darkness. Eliam tossed wood on the fire and poked it with his staff, but his eyes turned back to

Jonah, awaiting his answer. Jonah took a deep breath and tried to tell the story in as few words as possible.

"I was a prophet, rather I am a prophet. The Lord called me to take a message of judgment to Nineveh. I could not bring myself to carry that message. I feared the Lord might be as merciful to those wicked people as He was to Israel during her times of wickedness, even as He is today. I see how our nation is. I see the evil of King Jeroboam and his disregard for God, yet the Lord sent me to tell him that Israel's borders would be expanded. The ways of the Lord are sometimes difficult to understand. He shows mercy where I would send down fire from the sky."

"When God called me to go to that wicked city of Nineveh, I could not bring myself to go. Who knows, the Lord might cause them to change their hearts. If I knew every one of those vile people would die at the hand of God's judgment, I would run as swiftly as my feet could carry me and proclaim their certain destruction. But I know God, and I feared He might spare them, so I ran. I got on a boat bound for Tarshish. My foolishness almost cost the sailors their lives. It was an awful storm sent from the Lord. Had those men not thrown me overboard, we would have all perished together. But God saved them from the storm and saved me from the depths of the sea. He was merciful to me and delivered me by sending a great fish to swallow me." At this, the mouths of both the boy and his father dropped open.

"Yes, a fish," Jonah continued. "He spit me up on the shore, and now He has told me again to go to Nineveh. What else can I do? I will go, and may the Lord see their wickedness and do to them what He did to Sodom."

Jonah abruptly changed the subject, "I am in debt to you for your hospitality, but I beseech you to not ask anything more. I will leave you in the morning, and I will pray that you will be set free from your bondage to return home with your son."

Eliam motioned to his son, who got up and showed Jonah to a small shelter beside the olive grove. The pillows from the house were placed on a cloth on the dirt floor of the shelter. There was water and food inside.

Jonah patted the boy on the shoulder and lay down on the pillows. The young boy turned back after a few steps and stared intently at Jonah. "A fish?" he asked with childlike wonder.

Jonah gave him a small smile and spoke softly, "Yes, I was eaten by a fish." The boy's eyes were wide as he turned to go back to his father. Jonah adjusted the pillows and settled in. He was asleep in a matter of moments.

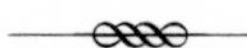

The next morning Jonah woke to the sound of a donkey braying. The sun was high in the sky. He did not know how long he had slept, but he didn't see any sign of Eliam or his son. He did see that a donkey was tied to the nearest olive tree, a blanket was thrown over its back, and it loaded with supplies. Lying on the donkey's back was a clean robe. Near Jonah's feet were a basin of water, a towel, and a pair of sandals.

He rose, washed himself, and changed clothes. He ate some of the dates and bread that had been left in the shelter. Jonah called to Eliam and to the boy, but there was no answer. He checked the house; it was empty. He figured that they may have taken olives to market, or it could be they were deep in the grove.

Jonah walked to the donkey and stroked its nose. This was a great kindness shown by a fellow Hebrew. It was undeserved, an act of mercy, and Jonah was grateful. Still weak from his three-day ordeal, he willed himself to climb onto the donkey. Jonah grabbed the rope and turned the donkey's head to the east. The beast responded, and they began to journey in the direction of Nineveh.

11

The Great City

The storm and the fish seemed so very long ago. Leaving Abidan seemed even longer. Jonah felt as if he had aged a hundred years since last seeing his son's face. He looked at his hands; they were still pale from three days in the fish's belly. Jonah was certain he looked like some kind of unearthly apparition and wondered as he traveled if he would ever fully recover.

He was weary from the long journey from Tartus. He had begun this portion of his travels with trepidation, but without fear. He had expected harassment. The closer he got to the great city of evil, the more likely some Assyrian dog would gut him just for the sheer joy of watching Jonah squirm and die.

Jonah considered that possibility. "Of course, so what if I am killed?" he asked himself. "It is no less than I deserve. And if I am killed, at least I would not have to preach to those dogs in Nineveh." But instead of abuse, Jonah found favor along the way from all he encountered.

He was provided with fresh water, food, and a place to lay his head at night. Not a day went by when he was not treated graciously. Perhaps, people were afraid of this man with pallid skin who seemed to carry a load of sorrow on his stooped shoulders. Jonah was a far different man from the bold prophet who had stood with shoulders back, chest forward, and head held high in the presence of the king of Israel and his court.

He had not always been so bold. As a boy, Jonah remembered he was dreadfully shy. Most of his conversations had been spoken as he gazed at the ground in front of his feet. He was easily embarrassed and had a hard time making friends. Despite all of this, Jonah's father had worked tirelessly to make a man of him. Jonah could almost hear his father's words: "Look me in the eye when talking. Don't mumble. Speak up as if what you say matters. This is not a world for the weak. Jonah, be strong. Be a man. Take a stand. Be bold, son. Be bold."

"Be bold." How many times had Jonah heard that statement? Whether it was because of an encounter with bullies or a simple conversation over dinner, his father would look him square in the eye and say, "Jonah, be bold."

Jonah wanted to be bold. It was not easy for him, but Amittai refused to give up on his son. Slowly, the lessons took hold, but it was not until Jonah was in his nineteenth year that boldness became his trademark.

Jonah remembered that it was a cloudless day as he worked his father's fields. The sun beat down on his bare shoulders as he pushed the oxen to finish their plowing before dark. He and his father had gotten up before sunrise to prepare the fields for planting. The next day was the Sabbath. They would certainly earn their rest.

The team of oxen plodded on ahead of him as his hands held the plow steady. The feel of soft, freshly turned earth passed beneath his feet, but Jonah's thoughts drifted to the face and form of a girl who had captured his heart. Her name was Yael. To say she was beautiful was to make the greatest understatement possible. He found his thoughts were increasingly of her. He was jarred back to reality when the oxen came to a sudden stop.

The oxen lay down as if preparing for sleep. It was an odd sight. This team was well-seasoned, and typically worked sunup to sundown without seeming ever to weary, but there they were, taking a mid-afternoon nap. As Jonah had searched for a stick he could use to motivate them, his eyes caught sight of a stranger in gleaming white robes who was standing in the shade of the big oak tree.

Forgetting his team of oxen, Jonah had made his way toward the man. He seemed harmless enough; in fact, he appeared to be friendly and welcoming. "May I help you, sir?" Jonah asked as he drew near.

The response from the stranger was startling, "No, Jonah, I am here to help you - and to burden you."

Immediately, Jonah had sensed the man before him was something more than a mere man. He averted his eyes and dropped his head. He felt a firm hand on his shoulder as the stranger leaned in to whisper near Jonah's ear, "The God of Abraham, Isaac, and Jacob, the Lord Almighty who created the earth and sea, He who is seated in glory sent me to you." Jonah held his breath as the words filled him with both fear and joy.

The man in gleaming robes continued, "Where God tells you to go, go. What God tells you to speak, you speak. Whether men listen or not, be bold. Be bold, Jonah."

As the sun was dropping below the horizon, Jonah had heard his name being called from far away. No, it wasn't far away; it just seemed so. "Jonah. Jonah, are you all right? Son, are you well?"

Jonah opened his eyes to see his father bending over him. Looking from side to side, he realized he was lying under the great oak where the gleaming man had stood. He strained his head forward to see the oxen resting right where they had been when he walked away from them.

"What is it, Jonah?" his father had asked with obvious concern.

Jonah had looked straight into his father's eyes and replied, "I think, no, I know - the Lord came to me."

With a mixture of both wonder and skepticism, Amittai had asked slowly, "And what did He say?"

Jonah smiled broadly at the remembrance of the visitor's words, "He said, 'Be bold.'"

The memory of his father's face faded into the brilliant blue of the sky before him. Jonah stopped his donkey and gazed ahead.

There it was, that expansive and wicked city standing brazenly before his eyes. The walls of Nineveh elicited an unwelcomed awe in Jonah. Even from such a distance, he had never seen anything like it. Carts likely carrying food and clothing for trade, lined the road leading into the large and well-guarded gate. Jonah could hear music carried by the breeze. It had been a long journey, but he was almost there.

He found a tamarisk tree and guided the donkey toward it. Dismounting, he tied his beast to a low-hanging limb. Jonah removed one of the skins and took a long, deep drink of the water. It was tepid but still quenched his thirst. He unrolled a blanket and spread it out in the shade of the tree. Turning his back to the city and facing the general direction of Jerusalem, Jonah prayed.

Prayer had been absent from Jonah's life since his decision to rebel. When he finally mustered the courage to pray, the words simply would not come. He had struggled to pray, but the closer he got to Nineveh, the more he found himself kneeling and praying. The Lord had not spoken to him since commanding him a second time to go to Nineveh. Even Jonah's sleep had been uninterrupted by dreams. It was as if the Lord was now waiting to see what His prophet would do. God had said all that needed to be said.

"Hear, O Israel, the Lord, your God, the Lord is one," Jonah began. He asked God's favor on Abidan. He prayed for Israel and for Jerusalem. With images of Yael drifting through his mind, Jonah prayed for the boldness to preach judgment in the streets of Nineveh. "Be glorified in their destruction, Lord. Amen." With his prayers finished, the determined prophet rose to his feet, rolled up his blanket and draped it over the donkey. He took one more deep swallow of water and remounted the animal. Turning his face toward Nineveh, he kicked the donkey's sides and began to move toward the very heart of human evil on Earth.

The closer Jonah came to the city, the more imposing the walls became. With every step the donkey made, the reluctant prophet felt as if he were shrinking. The city surely did not compare to the beauty of Jerusalem's gleaming walls, but the size was obviously intended to reflect the might of the Assyrians.

Nineveh sat on a rise. The Khoser River ran through the city, and wide channels had been dug around Nineveh, creating an additional barrier to confound any would-be invaders. Jonah crossed over two bridges leading toward the massive, reddish stone walls. A stone-paved, many-tiered ramp rose toward the eastern Shamash Gate between two great towers made of blue-tinted brick. Jonah's eye followed them from bottom to top. They seemed to reach to the clouds. The resolute prophet dismounted his donkey, took firm hold of the rope around its neck, and began the uphill walk into the city.

Soldiers in full battle array stood guard three deep on each side of the city gate. They were tall and expressionless, as if they were chiseled from the same stone blocks as the city walls. The presence of the guards was enough to tie Jonah's stomach in knots, but it was something else that drew Jonah's eyes and made him suddenly feel faint. The fierce sentinels stood in the shade of two enormous winged statues of the same half-bull half-man that had haunted Jonah's dreams for so long. The nearer Jonah came, the more he expected the creatures to come to life, exposing fierce, razor-sharp teeth dripping with blood, yet they remained still and lifeless. He took a deep breath as he prepared to step between the two bull-men.

Jonah's appearance caused the merchants and beggars lining the ramp to stop their activities and gawk at him. It was not his attire that drew their attention. He knew full well why they were staring; it was his exposed skin that captured the attention of the onlookers. Jonah was still an unearthly pale color, and the sun had caused pink and red splotches on his hands and face.

One of the guards stepped from his post and into Jonah's path. He scowled at Jonah and spoke words Jonah could not understand, a fact that seemed to amuse the guard. He turned to a deeply tanned and well-dressed man sitting on a pile of ornately patterned cushions. His white robe was embroidered with the same winged sun emblem that was carved above the gate. The guard spoke something to him. The man was likely a city official responsible for those coming and going through this gate.

The official reluctantly rose from his place and walked over to Jonah inspecting him from head to toe as he drew near. He spoke, but again the words were lost on Jonah. The man tried twice more to communicate, offering different phrases; Jonah only shook his head. "Hebrew," Jonah offered.

The official's nod changed from side-to-side to up-and-down. He responded, "Hebrew?" Then, he offered an awkward version of "Shalom."

"What is wrong with you?" the well-dressed Ninevite asked. Without touching Jonah, he drew his face close to examine this stranger more closely. He sniffed at him. "Are you sick? If you are sick, you cannot enter. Go away."

There was no simple explanation for his situation, so Jonah didn't bother to try. If he died here in the gate from the point of the guard's spear, so be it, but he would not die without speaking God's message.

Jonah rose to his full height, seemingly throwing off a heavy burden on his shoulders. He looked straight at the official and spoke with a surprisingly strong voice that carried above the din around him, "Thus says the Lord God of Israel, in forty days Nineveh will perish."

The official staggered back. The guard who was nearest to Jonah looked as if he'd been punched in the gut. This was not the reaction the prophet had expected. The old zeal that once coursed through Jonah seized him once more. He turned his back to the guard, a move he would normally consider to be unwise, but, caught up in the moment, caution was not foremost on his mind. He waved his blotchy hand back and forth and shouted to those on the ramp below him, "The Lord God of Israel has declared this wicked city will be destroyed in forty days."

Jonah turned on his heels, filled with a renewed strength. No one moved to stop him as he strode purposely through the gate.

The official raised a hand and opened his mouth as if to say something, but no words came.

The reenergized prophet noted the thickness of the walls as he passed through the gate, pulling the donkey behind him. No wonder the people felt secure here. Who other than the Lord could bring these dogs to their knees? A slight smile crossed Jonah's face as he imagined the gates torn from their frames and the city ablaze with God's judgment.

As he passed from the cool shade of the gate into the city, Jonah was overwhelmed with the sheer size of the place. There were people everywhere. Music played from a hundred different directions. There was laughter, shouting, the sounds of children playing, and the bartering of merchants selling their wares. Ribbons of smoke from cooking fires traced upward like snakes climbing to the clouds. Shops and houses bordered wide streets and lined the city's inner walls. Channels flowing with fresh water fed lush gardens. Straight ahead, Jonah saw what he imagined to be a temple, or perhaps it could be a palace. He would find out for sure soon enough.

Jonah thought that, perchance, somewhere in this city was the man with Yael's blood on his hands. Although he would not admit it even to himself, Jonah knew deep inside the words of judgment he would bring to Assyria's wicked capital would be more than a mere concession to God's call. It would be a death sentence for those who had taken his beloved wife.

Jonah let go of the donkey's rope; it would either be taken by someone who felt their god had smiled upon them or left to wander aimlessly into one of the gardens, where it might find some much-needed rest and refreshing water to drink. He turned to his right and began to walk the wide, paved street that followed along the city's wall. His message was simple. It was spoken with passion but without compassion: "In forty days Nineveh will be destroyed!"

Men stepped out from their shops to see what was happening. Women peered out from windows to hear the voice rising above the city's usual noise. Conversations stopped as people turned toward this pale prophet who yelled in a language unknown to most and pointed his finger intermittently at one person then another.

It did not matter to Jonah if they understood him or not. He had not been commanded to make them understand nor to call them to repentance; he was only to preach his message of judgment, and he did so with vigor.

A crowd began to follow Jonah as he continued his mission. He heard an occasional jeer, or what he assumed was jeering, directed at him. He barely dodged a nasty mixture of urine and feces tossed from a second-story window. Many in the throng following him laughed at the gesture of disrespect. Jonah ignored it. It was not the first time he had been criticized or threatened. He had a renewed boldness, for he was certain he would have the last laugh.

By the time the sun was setting against the western wall, Jonah had covered nearly a third of the city, weaving through the streets and pausing to drink from the fountains when he became thirsty. The crowds had now retreated to their homes for the evening to share with their families the activities of this odd foreigner who raged and stormed through their city streets. A few of Nineveh's citizens lingered a short distance from Jonah as he sat on a low wall, removed his sandals, and plunged his feet into gently flowing canal. They spoke in low whispers, and Jonah wondered if they might be planning to attack him once darkness engulfed the city.

As Jonah looked intently at the small, whispering mob, he was startled by a voice behind him. As he turned in the direction of the words, he realized they were spoken in Hebrew! "My master requests that you come to his home tonight," spoke a young man. The man held a rope in his hand, and on the other end of that rope was Jonah's weary donkey. "Will you come?"

This was wholly unexpected. Hearing flawless Hebrew was not nearly so surprising as finding hospitality in Nineveh. "Who are you?" Jonah asked. "And who is your master?"

"I am Ammon, son of Jacob, from the tribe of Reuben. My master is Sharrukin. He sent me from the eastern gate. You encountered him earlier, I understand. Will you do him the honor of staying in his home?"

Jonah pulled his feet from the canal and reached for his sandals. Ammon dropped the rope and raced over to Jonah, reaching for the sandals in order to place them on Jonah's feet. "No!" insisted the tired prophet. "You may be forced to serve a Ninevite, but you will not be forced to serve me. I will go with you for your sake, but to stay in the house of an Assyrian dog…" His words trailed off to nothingness.

When Jonah had tied up the leather straps of his sandals, he walked over and took the donkey's rope from Ammon's hand. He fell in behind the young man, and they weaved through a number of narrow alleyways and ended up on a broad street dimly lit by torches on each side. Jonah looked at the street in the flickering light. He noted how detailed the stonework was. Inset into the roadway, using brightly colored stones, were the images of fish spaced out at consistent intervals. "Fish," thought Jonah. "I thought I'd seen the last of them for a while."

At the end of the street was a spacious house standing three stories and painted in rich blues and greens. Jonah heard the sound of children's laughter from the upper floor and smelled roasting calf. Four well-armed guards stood at the door, but they made no move to intercept Jonah as he drew closer. At the door, Ammon took the donkey from Jonah as a man in a simple white robe stepped through the doorway and bowed. His face was easily recognizable.

Sharrukin spoke in faltering Hebrew but with a reverent tone, "I am honored that you came. I ask humbly that you eat with us and show kindness to us by staying as my guest. Your needs will be met. I ask nothing from you but your company," he hesitated, "and to hear more of this message you bring from the Hebrew God."

The official stepped back and motioned for Jonah to enter. Inside the prophet a debate raged. This was not what he had expected, and he was not sure it was what he wanted. Sharrukin seemed genuinely interested to know more of the Lord's message. He closed his eyes and breathed out a deep sigh. For the sake of his fellow Hebrew, he chose to accept the official's offer.

Slowly, Jonah eased into the well-lit room. Never had Jonah seen so many riches on display. Even Merari at his wealthiest could not have come close to comparing with this. Gold shimmered in the lamplight. The floors were covered with intricately woven rugs. Purple and red curtains hung on the walls, and well-stuffed pillows were stacked neatly in the corners. This was a man of means and influence. Jonah did not fear him, but he was wary of his motives.

A servant girl came with a basin of water. Even the basin was covered with colorful designs, and the towel was a brilliant white, rivaling the robe worn by Jonah's host. Jonah prepared himself to decline the offer of a servant washing his feet and was startled when Sharrukin himself took the basin from her. He motioned for Jonah to sit on the high stack of pillows near the door, untied Jonah's sandals, and gently but thoroughly washed the prophet's feet. Like his hands and face, Jonah's feet were also a splotchy pink and white as the heavy dust and dirt was washed away. A pair of red and blue slippers was offered to Jonah, but he declined by waving his hand. Sharrukin helped the prophet to his feet, and they made their way to the stairs at the back of the house.

The upper floor of the house had large windows with an expansive view of the city. Jonah's face was caressed by a gentle breeze. Sharrukin introduced his wife and four children, the youngest child, Ninu, was four, and her smile began to chip away at Jonah's hardened heart almost immediately. She innocently poked and pulled at his skin as if it were a garment Jonah was wearing. Sharrukin tried to stop her, but Jonah, with a quick gesture, waved him off. Perhaps it was her innocence that touched Jonah, but Jonah knew there was something more; it was her eyes, her emerald eyes, the eyes of Urmitu.

When the servants came in with the feast, Sharrukin's wife gathered up her children and ushered them to the stairs as the master of the house and his odd guest reclined at the low table. Jonah watched Ninu run to her mother's side. She turned and looked directly in Jonah's eyes. She spoke, and her voice was mature far beyond her age, "Chesed." Jonah was startled and jumped back.

Sharrukin was alarmed at Jonah's odd reaction. "What is it? Does something disturb you?"

"Your little one spoke to me, but her voice was," Jonah struggled to find the right word. "It was strange."

Sharruikin turned to the steps as Ninu's head of dark and tangled hair could be seen descending. "I heard nothing odd. What did she say?" inquired Sharrukin with a look of concern on his face.

Memories of Urmitu flooded Jonah's mind. He could see her eyes, eyes so very much like Ninu's. It was not the voice of a small child Jonah had heard, but the voice of Urmitu, and perhaps, he thought, the voice of God to him.

He closed the door on this part of his mind. He did not want to think about mercy, not for these people and not for his host, not even for Ninu. As he settled down deeply into the pillows, he dipped his hands in the bowl provided for washing. Jonah took some of the food from the bowls set before him, and then looking around, he asked, "Where is the Hebrew servant Ammon?"

Sharrukin spoke to a servant nearby with a torrent of quick words completely unintelligible to Jonah. The servant immediately turned and headed down the steps shouting orders as he went. Sharrukin smiled at Jonah. The smile seemed to be genuine and almost apologetic. "How thoughtless of me. I have asked for Ammon to clean up, change clothes, and join us. I am sure it is good to have one of your people here. He is a good and faithful servant. He still worships the Hebrew God. He will not even enter the temple with me when I go to make my sacrifice."

Jonah refused to eat until Ammon appeared. It was not long before the Hebrew servant rushed up the stairs, his hair wet from bathing, and stood before Sharrukin. He bowed first to his master, and then bowed deeply and reverently to Jonah. As he arose, his eyes fixed on Jonah's; they were filled with hope and expectancy. Ammon then moved to the pillows that had been placed at the table by an older servant who then stood quietly in a corner, awaiting whatever command might be given him.

"A raiding party captured Ammon some years ago," Sharrukin broke the silence. "I found him in the slave market. He was badly beaten, thin, weak, covered with bruises and cuts. I would have walked past, but my wife, she has a tender heart." He paused. "She insisted we purchase him, and that he would be a good servant to add to our household as we moved into our new home. You see, I had just been given a position over the king's guard and with it came this place." Sharrukin gestured broadly with a sweep of his arm. "My wife has proven to be quite wise. There is no servant in the household more trusted than Ammon." A broad grin came over Sharrukin's face. "Once the fool almost got himself killed defending my honor."

Jonah bowed his head and offered a silent prayer of thanks for the meal even if he were eating in the wicked city of Nineveh. As he raised his head, he noticed Ammon was also finishing his quiet prayer.

The meal was both plentiful and excellent. Great care had been taken that nothing served would be unclean for this guest from Israel, one of the benefits of having a Hebrew in the household. The meat was tender and moist. The wine was sweet. No expense had been spared in setting out this feast. The household servants would eat well on what was left over.

When the meal was done, the servants came and cleared the table, leaving the wine behind. Almonds roasted in spices were placed on the tables, along with slices of fruit. The aroma was enticing, but they did not interest Jonah at the moment. His curiosity had been building during the meal. Why would this Ninevite, a man of power and influence, invite a Hebrew prophet to dine at his table and stay in his home, especially since Jonah's skin looked as if it were made of badly stained parchment? What was he after? What did he want from a Hebrew prophet?

"Why?" Jonah finally asked. The question hung in the air and seemed to confuse the host, who had just filled his mouth with a handful of almonds.

Sharrukin picked up his goblet quickly to wash down the nuts. Jonah had nothing to lose. With a stoic expression, he turned to Ammon and demanded, "Tell this Ninevite dog that I will not be bought with meat and wine. I will not be won over by a sweet child. I have no love for him or for his people or for his family. I am here to announce that God is going to destroy Nineveh. The great walls of this city are nothing to the Creator. The armies are but the play toys of children. He will not win the Lord's favor by treating me kindly. So why? Why has he brought me here?"

Ammon's eyes darted from Jonah to Sharrukin and back. It was obvious that Jonah had put him in an awkward situation, perhaps, even a dangerous one. "Go on," Jonah insisted, "tell him what I said - to the letter."

Ammon swallowed hard and relayed the prophet's angry words to his master. His tone was much calmer, but the impact of the words were readily apparent. Sharrukin's widened eyes revealed that nothing had been lost in translation. Jonah's eyes never left the Ninevite official, but it was not anger he saw; it was more like fear and astonishment. When Ammon finished, Sharrukin returned Jonah's gaze and spoke in his own tongue. He gestured to Ammon to translate after each phrase.

"I did not bring you here to win your favor. I brought you here to listen to your message. Prophet, I believe you. My nights are haunted by nightmares. They are filled with blood and screams and fire," Sharrukin hesitated as if recalling the images that accompanied his sleep.

"I was once in command of raiding parties," he continued. "We located caravans, stole what we wanted, and left no one alive to pursue us. We burned villages to ashes, took whatever treasures we could find, raped the women while the men and children watched, and then killed them all." Sharrukin's eyes became moist and his voice shaky. "I am not proud of this, but it was the only way that I knew. I proved a faithful soldier to the king, and he took note of me. I was rewarded with a position in his personal guard. During a brief revolt, I saved his life. As a reward, he made me his royal official in charge of the east gate and captain of the guard stationed there. Look around. I have everything I want, but I have no peace – not with the dreams."

"When you came and spoke to me at the gate, did you not wonder why I did not have you struck down instantly? How dare a Hebrew come here shouting at the king's guard and looking like some apparition? I did not have you killed because I had heard your message before, a thousand times over. In my dreams I hear 'Nineveh will perish.' And the voice," he paused and breathed deeply, "it is your voice I hear." He paused and drew a deep breath.

"Now, tell me, Prophet, is it true? Is there no hope? Ammon has told me about your God, a God who speaks and His very words caused the sun and moon and stars to form, a God whose voice can shatter mountains, whose breath can part seas, and whose face shines brighter than a thousand suns. The earth has quaked violently under our feet in recent days. The King's advisors tell him this is a sign that the gods are displeased, yet no sacrifice has stopped the shaking. And, now, even the king is having dreams of death and destruction"

"Ammon has told me of his God's power and of His judgments, but he has also told me of His mercy. Is it true?" Sharrukin's voice had a pleading tone, "Prophet, tell me, can there be mercy for a city so wicked as this one and for a man like me whose hands are stained with the blood of countless souls?"

A part of Jonah wanted to tell the whole truth, that God does forgive and restore, that the same God who judges also shows mercy, but Jonah had not come to share a message of mercy but one of judgment. He spoke slowly with eyes fixed on Sharrukin, "I was sent only to speak of God's judgment of Nineveh. In forty days Nineveh will perish."

Upon hearing the words, the official could no longer hold Jonah's gaze. His eyes dropped to his hands as if he were seeing blood drip from his fingertips. "Sleep well, Prophet," he spoke as he rose from the table. "Ammon will show you to your bed and stay near you there in case you need anything more." Sharrukin's slumped figure slowly descended the steps until he was out of sight.

Jonah awoke from his sleep. He had been given a bed on the roof. He had not slept so well in many days. A rooster was crowing in the courtyard next door. There was the smell of fires being started for the day and the sounds of women rousing their households as the first rays of sunshine could be seen somewhere beyond the eastern wall.

Wiping the sleep from his eyes, Jonah looked around discovering that Ammon was still sleeping soundly. He poured water from a pitcher nearby and drank his fill. His hand reached up and parted the thin mesh that protected him from insects. Jonah looked to find his sandals lying near the doorway; he slid into them and stooped to tie them securely. He still had a long distance to cover, so he had best get started.

He crossed the roof toward the stairs where a bowl of fruit waited for him. He chose an apple and a pear from among the assortment and slid them into the woven pouch over his shoulder. As he was about to descend the steps, a voice called out from behind him.

"Please wait," Ammon spoke. "My master has asked me to go with you, to ensure your safety. He has given me his signet ring to make sure no one harasses you. You are free to go wherever you will. Perhaps the Lord will soften the hearts of the people here…" His words and the faint hope they contained trailed off as Ammon looked at the stern expression on Jonah's face.

Ammon then rolled from his bed and quickly tied his sandals around his feet and ankles. He splashed water on his face from the basin beside the bowl of fruit. Ammon picked up an apricot and bit into it, the juice trickling down his beard. Wiping at the juice with his sleeve, he chose two more apricots and a bunch of grapes and fell into step behind Jonah.

The large house was quiet as the two made their way to the first floor and out into the street. Jonah turned his head both ways to get his bearings. He headed toward the garden where he had first met Ammon. The determined prophet would begin at that spot preaching the same message he had the day before. Jonah paused and looked upward. The prayer was barely audible. "Lord, God of heaven and earth, fill me with your Spirit that I might faithfully proclaim Your word. Show these people Your judgment."

Jonah's eyes shifted to the street in front of him, and he took the first of many steps that day.

By late afternoon the crowds had begun to follow close behind Jonah. Few of them could understand his words, but news about this pale Hebrew and his message of doom had spread rapidly throughout the city. There was some jeering and cursing from those assembled, but most had worried looks on their faces. Some women gathered in groups, crying loudly. A number of shops had closed. A few families were packing large ox-drawn carts, as if they were leaving the city. None of this was what Jonah expected, and he was not certain it was at all what he had wanted.

Jonah traveled the streets and alleyways proclaiming his message of the destruction to come. Children seemed frightened by his appearance, but the adults seem to fear something else. The more his route took him inward toward the king's palace and the large, ornately adorned temple standing near it, the more Jonah noticed cracks in the buildings and walls. A few structures had collapsed and were in the process of being repaired. "This must have been caused by the earth's violent shaking," Jonah thought, remembering the words of Sharrukin. "God has already been giving them a foretaste of the judgment to come."

Ammon grasped Jonah's shoulder from behind and bowed his head as the prophet turned toward him. "The people have asked me to ask you to pray for them." His words were hesitant and spoken meekly as if expecting Jonah to strike him for relaying such a message. Jonah did not strike him; instead, he squinted past Ammon, looking intently into the crowds that gathered. The angry scowls and clinched fists he had seen the day before were gone. Many eyes glistened with tears. A group off to his left were wearing rough, itchy sackcloth. It was obvious they had dumped ashes on their heads. These people stretched their hands to heaven and groaned as if in deep pain. Jonah strained to understand what they were saying above the buzz of a thousand voices. He could only understand one word, and that word caused Jonah to turn cold and begin to shake.

The Ninevites were calling out the name of Yahweh.

Sharrukin did not come home for dinner that night. Ammon and Jonah ate together instead. The meal was much simpler, featuring rice, a mix of fruit, dates, and fish. Jonah decided to pass on the fish.

When the spiced dates were brought at the end of the meal, Jonah caught sight of a pair of green eyes peeking at him from the stairs.

"Ninu," Jonah called in a tender, grandfatherly tone. The girl was not shy. She scrambled up the steps and ran to Jonah. Her precious smile almost made Jonah forget where he was. The little girl pounced into his lap, causing Jonah to drop the handful of almonds he was holding. The nuts scattered like ants, and some bounced onto the floor. Ninu shrunk back as if expecting a sharp rebuke but none came. She looked into Jonah's face and, in place of a reprimand, received a gentle smile.

Ninu held up a black, carved animal to Jonah, obviously her prized possession. As she pulled it back from his face, Jonah could see it more clearly and wondered what type of creature it was.

"It's an elephant," Ammon chimed in. "They are quite common in Cush and beyond."

"An elephant," Jonah repeated. Although he had never seen one with his own eyes, he had heard of these creatures, massive animals that could rip trees up with their noses.

The girl placed the wooden toy onto the table and began to play with Jonah's beard. He picked the carved creature up and turned it over in his hands. It was stark black against the whiteness of his hands. It had obviously been carved with great care and was quite heavy for its size.

"Ninu!" a voice came from down the stairs. The girl shot straight up, leaped from Jonah's lap, and ran toward the stairs. After taking the first step downward, she turned and ran back. She gently took the small elephant from Jonah's hand, looked up at him with her beautiful emerald eyes, and turned to head back down the steps to answer her mother's call.

12
Repenting

With the rising of the sun on his third day in Nineveh, Jonah got up from his bed, washed his face, dressed, and grabbed some fruit from the bowl. His time in this wicked city was nearly over. As he descended the stairs with Ammon close behind, he found Sharrukin silently waiting for them. The king's official was no longer dressed in his regal finery but stood there in coarse sackcloth. Gone were his gold rings, and his feet were bare. His smooth olive skin was now colored a pale gray from ashes that had been heaped on his head. It was a sight familiar to Jonah, but not one he had expected from a Ninevite.

With head bowed, Sharrukin spoke to Jonah, "Prophet of the Most High God, our lord, the king requests an audience with you."

The Hebrew prophet could not have been more stunned if the king's official had informed him the king had turned into a hawk and flown away. He stood on the landing at the bottom of the stairs silently pondering what he had just heard. Kings did not request an audience; kings commanded an audience. Was Sharrukin simply softening the king's words? He did not seem the type to do so.

Jonah nodded in response and followed his host out the doorway. He looked for a royal chariot being pulled by ornately adorned horses that would carry them, but Sharrukin set out on foot.

Jonah noted immediately that the noises he had heard in the city the last two days were absent. The unexpected quiet was only broken by the sounds of loud, sorrowful wailing that drifted down from windows here and there.

As they walked, Jonah began to notice the few people passing by and those who sat in the lush gardens that they passed. Many of them were dressed in sackcloth, others in simple robes, and still others sat bare-chested. They sat in piles of ashes with ashes on their heads and shoulders. Face after face was streaked with tears. The sound of low whimpering and an occasional loud cry drifted through the nearly empty streets. He thought how strange it was that such displays of grief would take place in an area which, Jonah assumed, was usually filled with laughter and lively chatter.

Jonah's mind went back to his own experience of mourning over his nation, sitting in ashes, and crying out for the Lord to show mercy to His people. Were these people crying out to the false god Dagan or Ishtar? Or could it be they were crying out to the Lord? The very thought of it brought chills to Jonah; how dare their filthy, sinful lips utter the name of the Most High!

As they drew nearer to the palace, Jonah could hear the sounds of sheep and goats bleating. There was an enclosure for the animals up ahead, and in it, Jonah saw something he had never before seen even in Israel - the sheep and goats and even a few cattle had been covered with sackcloth, their heads sprinkled with ashes. What kind of display is this? Not even in Israel was repentance demonstrated in such a fashion!

Finally, they came to the heart of Nineveh where two massive structures stood, the king's palace and a temple dedicated to the false goddess Ishtar. At the entrance to both were the same colossal bull-men like those who stood as unmovable guardians of the city's eastern gate. But there was something markedly different about these statues; they had been draped with tent canvas hiding the statues' heads.

As they neared the temple dedicated to Ishtar, Jonah noted how it seemed to have a life of its own, built with blue-tinted brick and inlaid with the images of lions and dragons. As he followed

Sharrukin past the temple, Jonah saw the golden doors had been closed. For all its pretentious majesty, the place was abandoned and lifeless. Guards had taken their posts at the entrance to keep people out, and even they were wearing sackcloth and ashes.

Sharrukin was silent as the men walked. The only sounds were their footsteps treading the paving stones toward the king's residence. The palace, usually busy with officials and citizens incessantly coming and going, was oddly quiet. Guards stood at their posts, attentive but silent, alert but emotionless. Jonah followed Sharrukin and Ammon as they turned and made their way up a steep set of steps between the two covered statues. As Sharrukin took each step, ashes drifted from his head and shoulders.

As Jonah turned his head from side to side taking in this scene all around him, he noticed ashes had been scattered around the base of the bull-men. What kind of scheme was the king attempting? Was this true remorse or an attempt to deceive both the Lord and His prophet? Could it be true remorse? Jonah sought to erase that thought from his mind, but it stubbornly refused to stay away.

Through the open doors of the palace they marched until they came to two massive, gold-covered doors with intricate reliefs depicting some bloody Assyrian victory. The goddess Ishtar stood above the scene, bare-chested and smiling, as if offering her congratulations on the successful campaign.

The doors swung inward seeming to anticipate the trio's arrival. Guards stood aside with heads hung low. These once proud men seemed humbled as they, too, wore the unmistakable signs of repentance. The footsteps of the three echoed in the silent hall even though Sharrukin and Ammon wore nothing on their feet.

Jonah could not help but stare at the intricate carvings lining the hall and the inlaid tile floor that passed beneath his feet. He thought how peculiar it was that the room seemed to grow more and more dim with each step forward. He would have expected just the opposite as they neared the presence of he king.

A few paces from the steps that led upward to the throne, the men stopped. The prophet looked up expecting to see the king seated there in all his Assyrian glory. But there was no king. The throne was empty. The room was dark. Was this some sick attempt at humor?

Sharrukin had paused briefly, as if by sheer habit, but then moved beyond the throne room and into an adjoining courtyard. As they passed into the bright sunlight, Jonah's companions bowed. As Jonah's eyes adjusted to the light, he saw a man seated there on a heap of dirt and ashes. Around him were other men in the same piteous state. By all appearances, these could be a collection of common beggars gathered near some street corner. Each wore a coarse robe of goat's hair. The central figure did not look up but held his face in his hands. His shoulders heaved as he sobbed quietly. The backs of his hands showed the tracks of tears that had run between his ash-covered fingers. The most powerful king on earth gave every appearance of being a broken man.

Ammon stood still with his head lowered as Sharrukin moved forward and whispered something into the ear of the man seated in the middle of the grim assembly. As he stepped back, the King of Nineveh lifted his eyes. He was a pitiful sight to behold. Jonah's heart ached for this man but for only a moment as the anger and bitterness returned to assume their rightful role as protectors of Jonah's wounded heart.

As if to add salt to the king's wounds, Jonah spoke with all the harshness he could muster, "The Lord God says, 'In forty days Nineveh will perish.'"

The king did not speak; he merely picked up a piece of parchment lying beside him on the ashes and handed it to Sharrukin. The king's trusted official carried it to Jonah; a bit of ash fell from it and slowly drifted with the slight breeze. It was handed to Jonah. He stared at the words but could not read them. Ammon, who had moved close behind him, whispered, "Lord, may I?" and Jonah handed the sheet off to him.

Ammon held it in trembling hands and read the words very quietly to Jonah, "By the decree of the king and his nobles: 'Do not let people or animals, herds or flocks, taste anything; do not let them eat or drink. But let all, people and animals, be covered with sackcloth. Let everyone call urgently on God. Let them give up their evil ways and their violence. Who knows? God may yet relent and with compassion turn from his fierce anger so we will not perish.'"

Ammon's face showed a mixture of fear and wonder. The paper slipped from his fingers and drifted to the floor where it settled among the ashes. The act of letting a king's decree drop casually to the floor startled Jonah. It would be cause of immediate execution in any other similar situation, but the king took little notice of it.

"Am I to believe this is genuine repentance? Nineveh is no better than Sodom, no better than Gomorrah. It deserves the same punishment," Jonah spoke to Ammon, but he spoke loudly enough to be heard by those in the courtyard.

The king's look did not change. There was no hint of anger flaring up in his eyes because of Jonah's lack of respect in his presence. He simply spoke one word, a word that Jonah could not understand. The curious prophet turned to Ammon to receive the translation, but the young man kept his mouth closed. Had the king finally cursed the man who had declared the Lord's judgment on his iniquitous city? Had the king ordered his execution? Sensing Ammon's reluctance to deliver the translation, Sharrukin turned and spoke to Jonah, "He asks - for mercy."

13

The Angry Prophet and the Merciful God

Jonah had no words of comfort for the pathetic king. Why had he feared coming here? These were nothing but cowards and murderers deserving the worst that the Lord could bring against them. Let them beg for mercy. There would surely be none in this city.

Filled with righteous indignation, Jonah turned and left the courtyard the wind stirring the ashes into a cloud behind him. The wailing in the room intensified, but Jonah felt no pity. He walked past the king's empty throne and experienced something akin to self-satisfaction. As he strode back down the hallway to the great golden doors, the sound of wailing became ever more faint until it was lost in the vast hallways of the vast palace. Jonah could not help but think of Yael's tomb and of the grief he and Abidan shared. The judgment that would fall on these men was well deserved and would be total.

Without hesitation, Jonah exited the palace through the same door he had entered and stepped into the street. Nothing had changed. No guards were waiting to seize him and return him to the king's presence. He turned to go to Sharrukin's home to retrieve his donkey and depart from the city. His mission was complete. The sooner he left, the better.

Jonah opened the stall where the donkey was sleeping. He picked up the rope that was hanging on a wooden peg and nudged the sleeping animal that brayed and scrambled to stand. He placed the rope over the animal's neck, and Jonah proceeded toward the street. As he rounded the corner of the house, he caught sight of something or someone darting into the bushes on his right.

"Is someone there? Ammon, is that you?" No answer came, so Jonah stepped closer and pushed away the foliage. There he saw two emerald eyes gazing up at him. It was little Ninu, and her expression changed from alarm to delight when Jonah gave her a slight smile.

Ninu crawled out of the bushes and looked up at the pale man. Jonah placed his hand in her hair and gently stroked it. He thought of Abidan when he was this age. He thought of the innocence of one so small, and for the first time he felt pity for the fate of Nineveh, if not for the whole city, then at least for this one.

Her hand shot up and in it was the wooden elephant. She did not say a word but kept holding it up for Jonah. He reached down and received the little girl's prized possession. In the exchange, their hands touched. He wondered if the Lord might spare the likes of this one, but if this one, how many more? Ninu let go of her toy and smiled sweetly. She took hold of Jonah's legs and squeezed him affectionately. He felt as if something were melting in him at the child's touch. A few moments ago, Jonah felt so certain and self-satisfied at the city's doom, but now, as he gazed down into the shining eyes of this precious child, he felt a deep sorrow.

"Prophet," came a voice from behind him. Jonah tore his eyes away from Ninu and glanced over to see Sharrukin standing a few feet away. "Take the child. I deserve judgment. This city deserves judgment. But my little one, she does not."

"I cannot." Jonah pried Ninu from him and shooed her away as if brushing off an annoying fly. She looked confused but turned and ran toward the door of her house. Jonah was left standing face to face with her father. The prophet realized he was still holding Ninu's small elephant.

"Please," Sharrukin asked, his eyes pleading, "Have mercy. Take her." Jonah did not answer but stood perfectly still and emotionless.

Sharrukin straightened himself and swallowed hard. "Then take the toy to remember her. Having understood my own sin, I could not bear to watch Ninu play with it over the next forty days - not knowing how I came to possess it."

"I have heard my countrymen confess many sins this day. Even the king is listing every transgression he can think of in the hopes that your God might withhold his wrath from us. My sins haunt me, too, and that little toy is just a reminder. Do you know how I came to possess it?"

Jonah was silent, but Sharrukin continued. "I was part of a raiding party taking the goods from caravans and - rarely leaving anyone alive. I was ambitious. That attitude served me well, but it also has left me with great guilt this day. I had followed traders back to their little encampment. It turned out not to be as little as I thought. We attacked and killed quite a few men, women, and even a few youth. I found that elephant in the hands of a wounded man. I took it and was about to kill him when the tide of battle turned and we fled. You see, that little toy in your hand no longer represents a small victory and the bounty that came with it; it is now a reminder of the callous and wicked heart that beats in my chest. So, take it and go. In fact, take whatever you want." Sharrukin looked around at his grand home and well-kept grounds, and then dropped his head. "None of this matters. Not anymore." He then turned to follow his daughter into the house.

The little elephant seemed much heavier in Jonah's hand now. He tossed it into the sack slung over the donkey's back and started toward the street. He had not gotten far when he heard footsteps. Was it Ninu? Sharrukin? Some rogue guard coming secretly to take revenge on Jonah? He turned casually to see Ammon hurrying toward him with a sack thrown over his shoulder.

"Good," Jonah said delighted to see his fellow countryman. "You do not need to stay here and face God's judgment. Come. Let's go home."

Ammon secured the sack to the donkey and stepped back. "Here is some food, wine, and water for your journey, Prophet, but I am not going with you. I have prayed for a long time that my master would see my faith in the way I live. I will stay to pray for him, for this family, and even for this city. If God relents and chooses to spare Nineveh, then they will want to know this God of mercy. I will be here to tell them. If the Lord does not relent, then I will die with them, but, perhaps, some might even come to believe. Who knows? Perhaps, even the king himself."

Jonah opened his mouth to argue but could not find any words that made sense. He longed to have the same kind of hope that Ammon showed, but to embrace that hope would mean giving up his hatred of the murderers who stole the joy of his life and the mother of his son. He thought of Abidan's tears, of the ongoing burden of grief carried by Merari, and of Jethuel's limp that was a constant reminder of that one dreadful day. No, he would not change his heart, not for Ammon, not for Ninu.

Ammon gave Jonah a faint smile of assurance, and then turned toward the door of Sharrukin's house as Jonah turned toward the city gate. No shops were open. No children played in the streets. There were not even any guards at the gate. The city was exposed and vulnerable, but the people were far more worried about destruction from above than from any army that might storm the gates. The final sound Jonah heard as he walked past the pair of shrouded monoliths at the city's gate was the loud wailing of a woman atop one of the gate's towers.

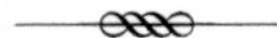

The donkey stumbled on loose rocks but kept her footing as Jonah guided her up the highest hill within sight of the city. He had delivered the message the Lord had instructed, but how would he know if God would follow through? The Lord was righteous and just, but He was also merciful. The wailing of the city's residents might invade the halls of heaven and stir His heart. Jonah would remain to see the promised destruction, as if willing it to happen would move the hand of God.

He had spoken first as he entered the city gates. Sharrukin had been first to hear it. By that calculation, Nineveh had thirty-seven days remaining, but Jonah determined that he would wait the forty full days to see what God would do.

As Jonah began the search for limbs and branches with which to build a small shelter, he was beginning to regret his choice of locations. Yes, the view of God's destruction of the city would be spectacular, but vegetation was sparse, and the final result of his effort of constructing a shelter was less than adequate. With some cloud cover it would be passable, but it would hardly provide sufficient shade on the hottest days. Jonah offered a quick prayer for cloudy and cool weather. He then sat down under his frail shelter and began his vigil.

A bit of food and water helped Jonah's mood. He also poured water for the donkey in a depression in the rocky soil. He wondered if there would be enough grass and foliage to feed the animal. Jonah sat and waited. No one came or went from the city. The only activity was the sight of a hawk gliding gracefully through the sky searching for prey. The only sound was the donkey's heavy breathing as she slept.

He watched the sun traverse its course across the sky until the purples and pinks of sunset were visible. Jonah sat there and marveled as God painted the sky in brilliant colors. He remembered how he and Yael used to sit and watch the sunset. He closed his eyes and tried to make the memory real, to feel Yael as she leaned into him, to smell the sweetness of her perfume, and to hear her voice as she whispered, "The Lord is so good to us - much better than we deserve." Jonah would always respond, "Yes, the Lord is merciful." As the memory faded along with the sunset, Jonah pulled a blanket up to cover himself. "Will you be merciful this time?" he asked, and he drifted off to sleep.

Sleep did not come easily that first night. After all the excitement of the last few days, Jonah thought he would cherish the solitude on the hilltop; instead he could already sense the boredom, and it was not even midday. Still, he would sit here and wait to see fire rain down from the heavens.

He stood and used his hand to shade his eyes from the bright sunshine. Jonah squinted toward Nineveh, but it was just as silent and still as it had been the day before. He turned scanning the horizon for any sign of change, but there was nothing.

The donkey's loud braying startled Jonah. He picked up a skin of water and emptied it into the depression to satisfy her thirst. As he watched the animal greedily drink its fill, he began to wonder if he might have to release her to fend for herself. Water would soon become an issue as Jonah waited and watched in the days to come. He took an apple out of the sack and took a bite. The sour taste surprised him. Had not the apples he had eaten in the city been much sweeter? He tossed it at the feet of the donkey who quickly consumed it and returned her attention to the water.

As he reached into the sack to fetch out something else to eat, his fingers landed on the little carved elephant. He took it out and turned it over and over in his hands. He marveled at the detailed work. Some skilled craftsman had surely taken his time with this piece. "An elephant," he said recalling its name. He remembered Ninu's small hands holding her special toy and Sharrukin's story of acquiring it.

His soul wrestled with his hatred of the man, and, yet, he felt some semblance of pity for him as a father who was about to lose what was more precious to him than his own life. As if to convince himself that his hatred of all Ninevites was justified, Jonah looked at the quiet city before him and said with all the conviction he could marshal, "A leopard cannot change its spots, nor can an asp change its bite."

Jonah set the trinket aside and continued to watch the city. He was surprised that it had not returned to normal activity. The bull-men guarding its gates were still covered. The smoke of cooking fires that once rose up like gray ribbons were no more. No merchant caravans lined up waiting to do their business in the city's streets. Nineveh was deathly quiet, as if inhabited only by ghosts. Jonah fully expected it would change. Once a few days had passed and no tragedy had befallen the ash-covered inhabitants, the people would resume business as usual. Merchants would once more ply their trades. Children would play in the streets. The king and his officials would feast and plan even greater atrocities on their neighbors. At the perfect time, disaster would come.

By day twenty, he had set the donkey free to try to scrounge for food and water. By day thirty, Jonah had run through his food stores except for some almonds and stale bread. By day thirty-eight, Jonah's water supply was gone. He was weary and bored. His only consolation was that the weather had been remarkably cool and that he had been spared the worst of the heat due to unexpected cloud cover. Jonah found he was having entire conversations with himself. For many days, he had talked to the donkey since she was his only companion. He had named her Ninu but noticed early on the beast of burden showed none of the affection that the donkey's namesake had shown. His exchanges with her had been unquestionably one-sided.

He passed the time trying to repeat the Scriptures he had memorized through the years. When he had exhausted that exercise, he tried to imagine every detail of Yael's face. In doing so, Jonah relived countless precious memories they had together. And the prophet talked to God, but the Lord remained silent.

It was day thirty-nine. Jonah woke with a combination of excitement and dread. When would the fire fall? Would God wait until forty days after Jonah left the city? When would he see his prophecy fulfilled? Jonah thought of home. When would he be able to return to Abidan? In the back of his mind, he worried if his prophecy would be fulfilled at all.

As the sun rose into a clear and cloudless blue sky, Jonah's miserable shelter provided little relief. Over the course of the last few weeks, the sun had dried out the green fronds and the winds had taken most of his covering away. Jonah sat underneath what remained, exposed to the intense heat.

He waited and wondered, and his wondering transformed into a deep, simmering anger. How dare God treat him like this! Jonah had always prophesied truth. What God told him to speak, Jonah spoke, and once spoken, the Lord brought that word to pass. If God did not soon destroy Nineveh, it would prove he was a false prophet. More importantly, if God did not destroy Nineveh, how could Yael ever rest in peace? How could he be at peace?

In a childish fit of rage, he lashed out at the few twigs and palm fronds remaining on the top of his shelter. He flung the debris in the air and shook his fist at the sky, "Lord, isn't this what I said when I was still at home? That's what I tried to forestall by fleeing to Tarshish. I knew that You are a gracious and compassionate God, slow to anger and abounding in love, a God who relents from sending calamity. Now, Lord, take away my life, for it is better for me to die than to live. Why don't You just kill me already? How could my life be any more miserable?"

Jonah sat down hard and folded his arms. An image of a pouting Abidan flashed through his mind, but he quickly closed that door and focused on the rage that swirled like a storm within him. Jonah stared intently at the city, thinking perhaps his anger would be the spark igniting a blaze that would consume Nineveh and everyone within its walls. He willed himself to push away the images of Ninu's innocent face, of Sharrukin's humble state, of Ammon's hope that somehow even the wicked king might come to worship God. Instead, he chose to focus on his anger and his desire for revenge, though somewhere deep inside he knew that the prayers offered in the city were sincere, and that the heart of the Lord had been moved to pity, an emotion Jonah would not allow himself to embrace.

As the sun rose higher, the heat became intolerable. Jonah's thirst made even swallowing difficult. A breeze began to blow, and Jonah turned his face to feel it. Perhaps his plight might be eased just a bit. He was wrong. The wind was not the cool breeze he hoped for but, instead, felt more like a blast from the mouth of a furnace. Jonah pulled his cloak up over his face. It would protect him from the sand, but it only made the heat more oppressive.

As he closed his eyes, Jonah heard something. It sounded like a voice. It started low but became clearer as the prophet focused on it. Jonah's eyes widened, and his grumbling ceased as he recognized it as the voice of the Almighty.

"Jonah. Jonah. Is it right for you to be angry?"

The question was incessant. It seemed to come with each blast of scorching wind.

"Is it right for you to be angry?"

Jonah wanted to respond, to stand, to turn his face heavenward, and to justify himself before God. He could not, however, bring himself to remove the cloth from his face or even to stand. He sat and gritted his teeth as the question replayed in his mind.

His weariness and frustration were shackles that weighed Jonah down. "Lord," he began, "end this now. I have done what you have asked. Either kill them or kill me. Either be merciful to them or be merciful to me. Just let this end."

As quickly as it had come, the voice was gone. Jonah lowered his robe from his face and noticed that the sun did not seem as intense. The winds, too, had subsided considerably. He dropped his cloak fully from his face and felt something unusual. It was shade. The prophet quickly turned his head and saw that somehow a vine had grown up on the remains of his shelter creating a canopy against the heat of the day.

"How…" Jonah started, but never finished his question. A small smile appeared on Jonah's dry and cracked lips. Was this the beginning of God's mercy? Was this a sign from the Lord that the destruction was indeed coming? Jonah took comfort in this and lay back to sleep the heat of the day away.

Tomorrow would be day forty.

By the time Jonah opened his eyes the sun had already risen. He stretched in an attempt to undo the stiffness he was feeling, but it was little help. "I'm getting far too old to be sleeping on the ground," he moaned to himself.

He stood slowly, then walked a few steps, leaned against a rock, and gazed at Nineveh. The city walls were as impressive as ever, yet it was still a place of mourning. It was day forty, and normal life had not resumed. Traveling merchants were turned away. From within the walls, only a few trails of smoke weaved their way skyward. It was as if the city had been deserted, but Jonah knew better. He had seen no mass exodus. They were all there, just as he had left them.

"Could these people truly be repentant?" Jonah wondered. "Had the message of impending doom been enough to convince the Ninevites of their weight of sin and cause them to repent?" The thought of it sent a chill through Jonah, but the chill was short-lived as the sun's heat beat on his neck. "At least there is the vine," he spoke softly and retreated to its shade.

Jonah crawled under his shelter and wiped the sleep from his eyes. As he settled in, his hand pressed down on something hard. It was Ninu's little elephant.

"So, little elephant," Jonah said as he picked up the toy. "Today's the day. What shall it be? Fire from heaven? Some vast army of angels? Perhaps the Tigris will overflow its banks and flood the city, choking the life out of every…" Jonah stopped.

He held the elephant above his head and noted how detailed the carving was. Suddenly, he remembered Ninu's hand as it brushed against his own. He could almost feel it. The thought of that smiling little girl with emerald eyes brought a smile to Jonah's face, and for a moment he considered taking Sharrukin up on his offer. Why should Ninu perish? What had she done?

He focused on the city gates, hoping to see the solitary figure of Ammon fleeing before destruction came. He hoped he would see Ninu being carried along in the young man's arms. But no matter how much he wished to see it, there was no movement.

"Ammon, you fool, do you really think you can persuade the dogs to follow the Lord?"

Jonah felt very weak and thirsty. Weariness washed over him, so he lay back down and looked up at the sky, blinking and squinting as the sun's penetrating rays poured in between the leaves on the vine. As he moved his hand up to provide a bit of shade for his face, he tried to recall whether his shelter was this thin previously. As he inspected the leaves that no doubt God had caused to grow up over him, he noticed they were wilting. Were the sun's rays that intense? It seemed as if he could almost see the life being drained from them.

Jonah scrambled to his feet and walked around his vine-covered shelter attempting to reposition the leaves. Many of them were dry and brittle to his touch. They easily fell off as he touched them, and the stiff breeze carried the loosened leaves away.

He examined more closely his sanctuary that had been provided so miraculously. It was then he noticed a small green worm munching away at the base of the stalk. Quickly, Jonah plucked off the squishy little pest. As he held it in his fingers, the problem with his vine was readily apparent; the worm had chewed clear through the stalk just above the ground depriving it of life. The vine was growing dryer and sparser with each passing moment. "What next?" he mumbled.

The worm still held between his fingers, Jonah retreated to what remained of his protection. As the sun moved in the sky, the grumbling prophet sat and moped as he stared at the little creature whose ability to destroy was far out of proportion to his size. All too quickly, the prophet's shade was gone, and the heat returned with a vengeance. "Enough with the games, Lord. My misery seems to be your objective here. Do you find some delight in this? You give me a plant to shade me then you send this - this worm to take it away. Why do you not just kill me and be done with it?"

Jonah found himself fuming with rage and not even caring it was directed toward the Almighty One. He dropped the little worm into the palm of his left hand and closed his fingers around it, intending to squeeze the life out of it. Was this not the immediate source of his misery? If he could not get back at God, this would perhaps bring a bit of satisfaction.

As his fingers began to tighten, Jonah stopped and opened his hand. "This little worm is not to blame for my misery," Jonah reasoned as he placed it on the dirt. "It was doing only what it knew to do, eating to survive. It could not know the misery it was causing to me or that it was destroying its only source of food." He watched as it wriggled away and retreated to the shade of one of the fallen leaves.

Jonah stood and walked around what remained of his shelter. He picked up a wineskin to take a drink of water. A sip was all that remained. It was not nearly enough to quench his thirst. He tossed it aside and began to pace, looking at the city of Nineveh in the distance, its walls still standing. As he paced, his anger grew. His steps became stomping. He kicked at rocks. "When will it happen? God don't do this to me! Don't let Yael's death go unpunished. Don't let the dogs who wander the streets of that vile city survive another hour. He turned his face upward, feeling the intense heat but not caring. "When, Lord, when?"

As soon as Jonah quit speaking, the wind ceased blowing, and an unearthly silence fell on the hilltop. Then, the voice of God spoke.

"Jonah, is it right for you to be angry about the plant?"

Without thinking of the consequences, Jonah spat his response, "Yes, it is! It most certainly is. My anger is fully justified for all I have lost and for how You have treated me." He knew he should stop speaking and humble himself before the Lord, but he could not. His words flowed from within like a raging river. "You show contempt to me but show mercy to those dogs in the great city there. I am angry! I am angry with all of this – angry enough to die!" Having exhausted his rage and readying himself for the Lord's anger to consume him, Jonah became quiet and held his breath.

Instead of the expected fireball from above, he heard a gentle voice. It was a tone very similar to that Jonah himself used when having to gently correct Abidan.

"My son," God began, "you have been concerned about this plant, though you did not tend it or make it grow. It sprang up overnight and died overnight. Should I not have concern for the great city of Nineveh, in which there are more than a hundred and twenty thousand people who cannot tell their right hand from their left - and also many animals?"

Jonah's mind flashed back to his three-day journey through Nineveh. Compassion was the farthest thing from his mind. The people of that city were all dogs worthy of the most painful deaths imaginable. He closed his eyes tightly to block out the images he had seen on the streets of Nineveh but to no avail. He could clearly see the city's pitiful king as he sat in ashes with tears streaming down his face. He could hear the wailing that poured from the windows of countless houses. He remembered the look of remorse on Sharrukin's face as he accepted that God's judgment was about to fall on him. Could it have been real humility, real repentance? No! How could it be? This was not why he came, but could it be why the Lord sent him? Deep down Jonah knew it to be true though he wished desperately that he could unknow it.

Jonah began to pick up rocks and hurl them in the city's direction. They only traveled a short distance, but Jonah imagined them as boulders destroying walls and flattening the whole place. He reached for another stone and was about to throw it when he realized it was not a rock at all. It was Ninu's elephant. He stopped. Somehow, Jonah could not bring himself to throw it. Instead, he pulled it back and looked intently at every detail.

He collapsed into a heap and wept bitterly. He cried for Yael. He cried for Abidan. He cried for Merari and for Jethuel. He cried for himself, for the man he had become. He cried for his rebellion. He cried for the hardness of his heart. He had become that which he most hated, a person without mercy and compassion, a person who followed his own path rather than the course set out for him by the Lord.

The sun was sinking on the other side of Nineveh when Jonah felt a hand on his shoulder. He turned to see a familiar face standing behind him. "Come, my Lord, eat and drink," the man spoke as he held out a skin of water for Jonah. The prophet was dazed, wondering if this were all his imagination.

"Ammon?" Jonah asked in confusion as much as recognition. Jonah turned his face back to Nineveh seeing that the city still stood. What was it he felt? Relief?

"My son, I have failed as a prophet. The wicked city still stands," Jonah spoke flatly.

"Failed? No, you have not failed! The people of the city call on the Lord. They have broken hearts and have turned from their evil. Sharrukin has freed me." A broad smile spread across Ammon's face. "Had you not come, these people would still be senseless worms. Now, they are thinking and feeling men. Come and see!"

Ammon's words were met with stunned silence. Jonah simply held on to the elephant and stared at the city.

14

The Return Home

Jonah did not set foot back in Nineveh. He sat on the hilltop throughout the night, and Ammon, somewhat concerned over the prophet's mental state, stayed quietly by his side.

Jonah spent much of the night weeping, sometimes with quiet whimpers and at other times with loud sobs. When he slept, it was fretful as if he were wrestling with an angel or perhaps a demon. Jonah would often wake with the word "mercy" on his lips. Sometimes it was spoken in a fearful tone and at other times as a tender plea. Ammon could only watch in awe of the disturbing sight.

When morning came, Jonah looked weary but more in control of himself. With his mind at ease over the prophet, Ammon rose to go back to Nineveh. He had chosen to remain with his former enemies in order to teach the truths of God. Jonah marveled at the hope radiating from the younger man. Jonah placed his hand on his young friend's head and blessed him. The two embraced, and then Ammon began his walk down the hill toward the great city that seemed more alive with many ribbons of smoke rising in the early morning sky and activity at its gates. For the first time in a long, long time, Jonah felt a peace in his spirit. His soul felt lighter. He sought to brush the feeling aside, but somehow it stubbornly remained.

Jonah gathered the sack of food and skins of water brought by Ammon and turned eastward to begin his trip home. It would be a long journey, and, he hoped, much less eventful than his journey to Nineveh had been. At the base of the hill he heard the sounds of hooves against rock. He turned to see the donkey he had named Ninu walking toward him. "Surely the Lord is merciful," Jonah said. The thought of using that term now caused him to laugh to himself.

Still smiling, he went over and placed his hand on the donkey's head. Retrieving an apple from his bag, he held it in front of the animal's mouth. After Ninu had enjoyed the treat, Jonah tossed his sack over her back and secured the skins. The weary but content prophet then climbed on, and the two of them began their homeward trek.

Jonah sat in the familiar setting of Merari's tent and waited for the old man to speak. His wife's father had listened to the story intently, not interrupting even once. Merari's face showed neither shock nor surprise.

"This is not right!" came an angry voice from Jonah's right. It was Jethuel who shifted on his pillows and was struggling to rise. His useless leg made his effort awkward, so Abidan rushed to his side to help him. "Am I to believe that the Lord forgave those dogs?" The words seemed to catch in his mouth. With a look of utter astonishment, he whispered, "Even the king?"

Before Jonah could respond, Merari broke his silence. Raising his hand to calm Jethuel, he spoke calmly to his son, "Are you higher than God that you may sit in judgment over Him? Each of us here has lost something precious - someone precious. Our hatred cannot bring her back; it simply poisons our souls."

"But, father," Jethuel shot back, "are we to forgive? How can we?" There was a hint of desperation in his question.

"I do not know, but I have listened to Jonah's story. Nineveh did not deserve mercy; that is true." Looking directly at Jonah, Merari asked, "My son, did you deserve to be spared though you ran from God? Did those sailors deserve to be spared though they were pagans? Did you deserve to be rescued by means of that great fish? I tell you, mercy is not deserved; it is received. I fear that if God were not merciful, we would all die very, very young."

The men finished their meal in silence. Each wrestled with the mysterious ways of God, the ever-present absence of Yael, and the wisdom spoken by Merari.

After excusing himself with a bow of his head, Jonah rose and went again to Yael's grave. Once there, he found his heart no less broken. Somehow he had expected it to be, given all he had been through. Nothing had really changed, nothing except Jonah's heart.

Though the absence of Yael still left an awful emptiness in Jonah, he was no longer filled with the intense hatred for the Ninevites. Each time he felt those fires stir up again within him, he thought of Nineveh's king weaping as he sat covered with ashes, he thought of Ammon's heart to teach the Ninevites the ways of God, and he recalled the innocent, emerald green eyes of Ninu. Though he still struggled with the words Merari had spoken after their meal, he knew the old man was right. The Lord is merciful even when we do not understand His ways.

Jonah brushed away a grasshopper and sat down on a flat rock, a place where he had grieved so many times before. He lifted his hands and offered a silent prayer for Ammon and Sharrukin and Ninu. As he lowered his hands, the fingers of his right hand fell upon the leather pouch at his side. He felt the outline of the small wooden elephant. Jonah untied the pouch and pulled out the little toy. As he turned it over in his hands, he remembered the wonder and innocence of the little girl who had touched his heart, and he regretted shooing her away after she put her greatest treasure in his hands. Jonah stood and walked over to the large stone in front of Yael's grave and placed the small figure in the sand in front of it.

He heard footsteps behind him and knew instantly they were those of Jethuel, assisted by Abidan. He wondered if Jethuel would ever accept God's attitude toward the Ninevites. His brother-in-law and friend had lost not only the use of one of his legs, but, far worse, he lost a sister who was slaughtered before his very eyes.

Jonah turned to face the two men. "She was my heart, as I know she was yours," he spoke tenderly to them. "I do not understand the ways of the Lord, but I have come to believe that He is right in all He does. I do not reject Him when He shows mercy to me. How can I reject Him when he shows mercy to others? Did the wicked Ninevites deserve mercy less than a rebellious prophet?"

Jonah stepped away from the tomb and closer to Jethuel. Yael's only brother sat with his head bowed and shoulders sagging. The weight of grief was obvious. He had heard both the words of his father and of Jonah, but mercy for Nineveh seemed impossible to fathom. As he lifted his eyes, they became wide. He blinked several times, as if trying to make sure what he was seeing was not a mirage.

Jethuel pointed a shaky finger toward the ground in front of Yael's grave. "That!" he whispered. "Give it to me." Jonah was confused by the request and was trying to figure out what Jethuel meant, but Abidan immediately understood and went over to pick up the dark carving on the ground. He brought it back to his wide-eyed uncle who held it in shaking hands. He said nothing; he merely looked at the toy with astonishment, tracing his fingers over every notch and curve.

As if trying to help Jethuel figure out a puzzle, Jonah said, "It's a gift from the little girl, Ninu. The one I told you about. What's wrong, brother? You look as if you've seen a ghost."

"Very close, I'm afraid," Jethuel answered. He lifted his head and looked at his nephew. Jethuel smiled, and a tear rolled down his cheek as he handed the little carving to Abidan. "I brought this home for you."

The Author

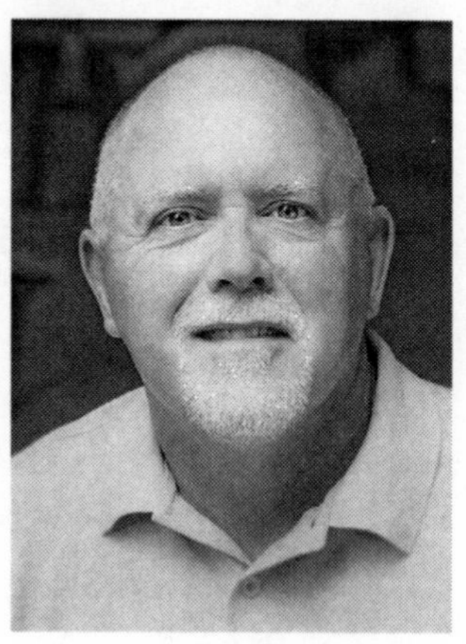

Jimmy A. Long is the founding pastor of Grace Fellowship of Greensboro, Georgia. He has served in full-time ministry since 1989. Jimmy is a graduate of the University of North Carolina in Chapel Hill, Southwestern Baptist Theological Seminary, and Southeastern Baptist Theological Seminary. He and his wife Nancy have two children, Jackie and Jay, who have grown up to love Jesus, family, and the church.